Effective Writing

Effective Writing

Anurag Sharma

ADHYAYAN
ADHYAYAN PUBLISHERS & DISTRIBUTORS
NEW DELHI (INDIA)

Published by
ADHYAYAN PUBLISHERS & DISTRIBUTORS
4378/4B, 105, J.M.D. House, Murari Lal Street
Ansari Road, Darya Ganj, New Delhi - 110002
Ph.: 011-23263018, 011-23277156, Fax: 011-23280028
Email: adhyayanpublishers@yahoo.com

Effective Writing

Edition 2011
ISBN 978-81-8435-288-7

Printed in India

Published by Harish Chandra Yadav for Adhyayan Publishers & Distributors, Laser Typeseting at A.V. Rao and Printed at Tarun Offset Printers, Delhi

Preface

Many of us find writing a tough and tedious task. Given a chance, we would slip away from the task. Everyone must learn to write effectively because, writing helps us explore our own thoughts and feelings. Writing forces us to articulate our ideas, to discover what we really think about an issue. Writing can provide a record of our thoughts that we would be able to study and evaluate in a way that conversation cannot.

On a more practical level, we need to write effectively to communicate with others. In school and college you have to write essays, tests, reports and exercises. Later, you may need to write formal letters of application for jobs, training programmes etc. And, on the job you may have to write numerous kinds of reports, proposals, analyses and requisitions. To be successful in any field, you must make your correspondence with business associates and co-workers clearly understandable. Writing enables us to communicate effectively with others.

Through today's mass media, we are continually bombarded with words from politicians, advertisers, scientists, preachers and teachers. We need to understand and evaluate what we are hearing, not only for our benefit but also for self-protection. Language is frequently manipulated to manipulate us. By becoming writers ourselves, we can learn to recognise and reject the irresponsible, cloudy, or dishonest language of others before we become victims of their exploitation.

An effective piece of writing is not just restricted to accurate grammar and spelling. This book describes the most important characteristics of effective writing. It includes good solid information for writers and would be especially useful for high school and college students.

Anurag Sharma

Contents

1

Writing of Plain English

Plain English means analyzing and deciding what information investors need to make informed decisions, before words, sentences, or paragraphs are considered. A plain English document uses words economically and at a level the audience can understand. Its sentence structure is tight. Its tone is welcoming and direct. Its design is visually appealing. A plain English document is easy to read and looks like it's meant to be read. Using plain English assures the orderly and clear presentation of complex information so that investors have the best possible chance of understanding it.

Getting Started

Select a Team

As with a lot of things in life, it's the preparation that often determines the success or failure of an effort to write documents in plain English. Many of you routinely select a team to think and talk about how to write a document from scratch or rewrite an existing document. Or you may do it on your own. In that case, rest assured that one person can do it alone.

The list below describes the types of people who have participated in successful plain English teams. We're not suggesting that you need to select everyone listed. Some will not apply to your company or your situation. The people you select, and the point at which you involve them in your plain English project, will depend on your document, your schedule, and your budget.

— A team leader who has the authority to make decisions that keep the project moving forward and bring it to a successful conclusion.The team leader may be a company's or an underwriter's lawyer.

— A lead writer who ensures the document uses a logical structure and simple, clear language. If more than one person is drafting sections of the document, the lead writer makes sure the final draft has a consistent tone and the individual parts form a coherent whole.

— Lawyers for the company or the underwriter who know what information must be included and why.

An investor relations expert who knows first-hand the financial sophistication of your investors. Investor relations people know which questions investors typically ask and where past disclosure documents have failed to make information clear.

— A compliance officer who can lend guidance to the writer and who knows, along with your lawyers, what information must be included.

— A production and operations person who understands the mechanics and costs of printing and mailing your document, so that your improved document doesn't get ahead of your in-house capabilities or budget.

— A marketing person who may have market survey research or polls on your investors. Also, the marketing department is usually attuned to the terminology that your investors can readily understand.

— An information designer who is a graphic designer trained to work closely with the writers and to think about how to present complex information visually.

Select Documents

You may want to consider these issues as you start writing in plain English:

— How long is the document?

— Will you write all of it, or only sections of it, in plain English?

— How much time do you have before you need to file your document?

You will also want to gather and distribute other documents that your company has written for investors. It's likely that your company has already used plain English in its glossy annual reports and other communications prepared especially for investors. These documents may save you time by showing you the type of language your company is already comfortable using.

Know Your Audience

Knowing your audience is the most important step in assuring that your document is understandable to your current or prospective investors. To write understandable documents, you need to gauge the financial sophistication of your investors.

Through polls and other market survey research tools, some companies know the demographical of their investors well. Other companies rely on their investor relations staff or their underwriters to describe who has bought, or is likely to buy, their securities.

Using whatever information is available, you can create a profile of your investors or prospective investors based on the following questions:

— What are their demographical age, income, level of education, and job experience?

— How familiar are they with investments and financial terminology?

— What investment concepts can you safely assume they understand? —How will they read the document for the first time? Will they read it straight through or skip around to the sections that interest them? —Will they read your document and your competitors' side by side?

— How will they use the document while they own the security?

What information will they be looking for later, and is it easy to find? Your investors or prospective investors may include individuals and institutions with varying degrees of financial sophistication. While your audience will include analysts and other industry experts, you may want to keep in mind that your least sophisticated investors have the greatest need for a disclosure document they can understand. Some companies have faced the differing needs of their investors and other audiences by making basic educational information visually distinctive from the rest of the text so that sophisticated investors can easily recognise and scan it.

Once you've drawn a profile of your investors, keep it constantly in mind. Some writers keep a photo of a typical investor to make sure they don't lose sight of their readers.

After analysing who your investors are, you can turn to the document

Know the Information You Need to Disclose

The steps outlined in this section have been used successfully by others who have written disclosure documents in plain English. Feel free to tailor these steps to your own schedule and team. This is one approach if you are rewriting an existing document, but others may work equally well.

Read and Outline the Current Document

Read the entire document once without making any notes or comments on the text. This should give you a general understanding of the information covered in the document and make your next read more productive.

When you read it the second time, make notes on what information is covered and any questions you have. Your notes will also help you to assess if information flows through your document in a logical order.

As you read, consider the following:

— Will the investors understand the language?

— Does the document highlight information that is important to investors?

— Is any important information missing?

— Does the document include information that is not legally required and will not help investors make informed decisions

Meet to Resolve Questions

Meet with the authors of the original document or others who understand it and any members of the team who can help to answer the questions you wrote in the margins. Besides the obvious reason for the meeting, another more important goal is to question the need for everything that appears in the document.

"Because it's always been there" is not reason enough to keep it in your draft. Since much of the language in these documents is recycled from older (or another company's) documents, often no one knows who initially wrote it or why it is needed now. If you've done your legal research and no one knows why the information is important or required, consider taking it out.

Eliminate Redundant Information

Question the need for repeating any information. Reading the same material two or three times can bore and even trouble readers. Most readers skip over paragraphs if they think they've read them before. If you cut down on repetition paragraphs or sentences, you'll not only earn the gratitude of your reader, you'll reduce printing and mailing costs.

Discuss the Cover page and the Summary

A cover page should be an introduction, an inviting entry way into your document, giving investors some key facts about your offering, but not telling everything all at once. If it looks dense and overgrown with thorny details, no one will want to pick it up and start reading. If it looks like a legal document written *by* lawyers and *for* lawyers, many investors will not even attempt to read it.

To create an inviting cover page, you'll need to strip away much of what is conventionally placed there, but which is not required. As you review your cover page, question why each item of information is there. It may be important, but does it have to be on the cover page? You usually have a substantial document following the cover page let some of those other pages carry the information load in logical order. What would be helpful for investors to see on this page? Look through your investors' eyes and you'll make better decisions about where to place information.

The same goes for the summary. A summary should orient the reader, highlighting the most important points that are presented in greater detail in the prospectus. Many summaries now seem as long as the document itself and consist merely of paragraphs copied straight from the body of the document.

Use defined terms sparingly

Although customary, introducing defined terms on the cover page and in the summary discourages many readers from getting beyond the first pages. Overwhelmed with memorising a new and unnatural vocabulary, and bothered by constantly having to flip back and hunt for the first time a defined term's definition appears, many an investor will not stick with the document. One plain English expert has advised, don't let a short-cut for the writer become a roadblock for the reader.

Reorganising the Document

A few principles of good organisation apply universally.

First, present the big picture before the details. Prospectuses routinely start with a detailed description of the securities. You may read pages before you find out what the company produces, or why it is merging or spinning off a subsidiary. It's hard to absorb the details if you don't know why they are being given to you. Imagine trying to put together a complicated jigsaw puzzle without first seeing the picture of the completed puzzle. An individual piece of information means more to your readers if they know how it fits into the big picture.

Second, use descriptive headers and sub headers to break your document up into manageable sections. Prospectuses impart a lot of information. If you present the information in bite-sized pieces, it's easier to digest. Make sure your headings tell the reader what the up coming sections will cover. Headings like "general" or "background" aren't especially helpful.

Third, always group related information together. This helps you identify and eliminate repetition information.

Fourth, your audience's degree of investment expertise will affect how you organise the document. If you are writing for financially unsophisticated investors, your document's overall organisation may take an educational approach. You may need to explain industry terms or concepts where they first appear.

Fifth, review your document by taking a good look at the flow of information from beginning to end. Start making decisions on how the content should be moved around into a new and logical order based on:

— the audience profile
— the notes you made in the margins
— the decisions you've made on your cover page and summary
— the information you've learned in answering your questions

Once you have finished physically reorganising the document, you may want to write an outline of your new organisation. Your outline can later become your table of contents.

Problems in Writing in Plain English

The most common problems we've encountered with disclosure documents.

Common Problems

1. Long sentences
2. Passive voice
3. Weak verbs
4. Superfluous words
5. Legal and financial jargon
6. Numerous defined terms
7. Abstract words
8. Unnecessary details
9. Unreadable design and layout

Using the Active Voice with Strong Verbs

The plodding verbosity of most disclosure documents makes readers yearn for clear words and short sentences. The quickest fix lies in using the active voice with strong verbs. Strong verbs are guaranteed to liven up and tighten any sentence, virtually causing information to spring from the page. When you start to rewrite or edit your work, highlighting all the verbs can help.

The time you spend searching for a precise and strong verb is time well spent. When a verb carries more meaning, you can dispense with many of the words used to bolster weak verbs.

Weak verbs keep frequent company with two more grammatical undesirables: passive voice and hidden verbs. In tandem, they add unnecessary length and confusion to a sentence.

Active and Passive Voices

If you need it, here's a quick refresher on the active and passive voice.

Active: The investor buys the stock.

In the active voice, the subject of the sentence, the investor, performs the action, buying the stock.

Passive: The stock is bought by the investor.

In the passive voice the subject, the stock, is acted upon. The person or the thing doing the action is introduced with "by." But sometimes, the person or thing doing the action is deleted, leading to...

Passive with agent deleted: The stock is bought.

You don't know who bought the stock. You'll find many examples of the "passive with agent deleted" in disclosure documents.

Readers understand sentences in the active voice more quickly and easily because it follows how we think and process information. Many times the passive voice forces readers to take extra mental steps as they convert the passive into the active.

To recognise the passive voice, ask yourself:

Does the sentence use a form of the verb "to be" with:

1. Another verb in the past tense; and
2. A prepositional phrase beginning with "by"?

Remember that it's harder to recognise the passive voice when the object is left out. When you rewrite the sentence in the active voice, use a strong verb. These examples show how strong verbs and the active voice transform sentences, making them shorter and easier to understand.

Before: The foregoing Fee Table *is intended* to assist investors in understanding the costs and expenses that a shareholder in the Fund will bear directly or indirectly.

The before example uses the passive with agent deleted. We don't know who "intended" to assist investors. Note how long it took to get to the meat of the sentence. Dispensing with the filler words "...to assist investors in understanding..." Moves the reader more quickly to the important points.

After: This table describes the fees and expenses that you may pay if you buy and hold shares of the fund.

The plain English version tells you who may revoke a proxy and where to find the information on how to do it. It replaces the abstract "subject to the procedures described herein" with concrete, everyday words, "by following the directions on page 10." It's not enough merely to translate existing texts—the key is to add useful information.

Using Passive Voice Sparingly

The passive voice may make sense when the person or thing performing the action is of secondary importance to another subject that should play the starring role in sentence. When in doubt, choose the active voice.

Find Hidden Verbs

Does the sentence use any form of the verbs "to be," "to have," or another weak verb, with a noun that could be turned into a strong verb? In these sentences, the strong verb lies hidden in a nominalisation, a noun derived from a verb that usually ends. As you change nouns to verbs, your writing becomes more vigorous and less abstract.

Personal Pronouns

No matter how sophisticated your audience is, if you use personal pronouns the clarity of your writing will dramatically improve. Here's why.

First, personal pronouns aid your reader's comprehension because they clarify what applies to your reader and what applies to you.

Second, they allow you to "speak" directly to your reader, creating an appealing tone that will keep your reader reading.

Third, they help you to avoid abstractions and to use more concrete and everyday language.

Fourth, they keep your sentences short.

Fifth, first- and second-person pronouns aren't gender-specific, allowing you to avoid the "he or she" dilemma. The pronouns to use are first-person plural and second-person singular.

Bring Abstractions Down to Earth

Abstractions abound in the financial industry. What pictures form in your mind when you read these phrases: mutual fund, the Dew Johne's Industrial Average, zero coupon bond, call option, or foreign currency trading? It's far easier to comprehend a concept or a situation when your mind can form images.

In a study conducted at Carnage-Melon University, a cognitive psychologist and an English professor discovered that readers faced with complex written information frequently resorted to creating "scenarios" in an effort to understand the text.

You can make complex information more understandable by giving your readers an example using one investor. This technique explains why "question and answer" formats often succeed when a narrative, abstract discussion fails. Although it is impossible to eliminate all abstractions from writing, always use a more concrete term when you can.

The following examples show how you can replace abstract terms with more concrete ones and increase your readers comprehension:

before: Sandy hill Basic Value Fund, Inc. seeks capital appreciation and, secondarily, income by investing in securities, primarily equities, that management of the Fund believes are undervalued and therefore represent basic investment value.

After: At the Sandy hill Basic Value Fund, we will strive to increase the value of your shares (capital appreciation) and, to a lesser extent, to provide income (dividends). We will invest primarily in undervalued stocks, meaning those selling for low prices given the financial strength of the companies.

Before: No consideration or surrender of Beco Stock will be required of shareholders of Beco in return for the shares of Units Common Stock issued pursuant to the Distribution.

After: You will not have to turn in your shares of Beco stock or pay any money to receive your shares of Units common stock from the spin-off.

Omitting Superfluous Words

Words are superfluous when they can be replaced with fewer words that mean the same thing. Sometimes you can use a simpler word for these phrases:

superfluous	***simpler***
in order to	to
in the event that	if
subsequent to	after
prior to	before
despite the fact that	although
because of the fact that	because, since
in light of	because, since
owing to the fact that	because, since

Another source of superfluous words is "shotguns": letting loose a blast of words hoping at least one conveys your intended meaning. The simplest solution here is to replace your laundry list of adjectives with a single word or phrase that adequately expresses your intended meaning.

WRITE IN THE "POSITIVE"

Positive sentences are shorter and easier to understand than their negative counterparts.

Also, your sentences will be shorter and easier to understand if you replace a negative phrase with a single word that means the same thing. For example:

negative compound	*single word*
not able	unable
not accept	reject
not certain	uncertain
not unlike	similar, alike
does not have	lacks
does not include	excludes, omits
not many	few
not often	rarely
not the same	different
not ... unless	only if
not ... except	only if
not ... until	only when

USE SHORT SENTENCES

No one likes to read a sentence that's two pages long. And yet, lengthy, information-packed sentences choke many prospectuses today. To complicate matters further, these sentences are filled with jargon and legalese. The longer and more complex a sentence, the harder it is for readers to understand any single portion of it.

Information-packed sentences leave most investors scratching their heads. So many of these sentences have become "boilerplate" that writers cut and paste them into new documents without thinking about how they can be improved. Since these sentences can be a little intimidating, we thought we'd tackle another one:

Before: The Drake Capital Corporation (the "Company") may offer from time to time its Global Medium-Term Notes, Series A, Due from 9 months to 60 Years From Date of Issue, which are issuable in one or more series (the "Notes"), in the United States in an aggregate principal amount of up to U.S. $6,428,598,500, or the equivalent thereof in other currencies, including composite currencies such as the European Currency Unit (the "ECU") (provided that, with respect to Original Issue Discount Notes (as defined under "Description of Notes—Original Issue Discount Notes"), the initial offering price of such Notes shall be used in calculating the aggregate principal amount of Notes offered hereunder).

After: The Drake Capital Corporation may offer at various times up to U.S. $6,428,598,500 worth of Global Medium-term notes. These notes will mature from 9 months to 60 years after the date they are purchased. We will offer these notes in series, starting with Series A, and in U.S., foreign, and composite currencies, like the European Currency Unit. If we offer original issue discount notes, we will use their initial offering prices to calculate when we reach $6,428,598,500.

As you can see, one long sentence became four shorter sentences. The paragraph moves from the general to the specific, contains short, common words, and is written in the active voice. You only need to read the paragraph once to understand it.

Replace Jargon with Short, Common Words

Ruthlessly eliminate jargon and legalese. Instead, use short, common words to get your points across. In those instances where there is no plain English alternative, explain what the term means when you first use it.If you have been in the financial or legal industry for awhile, it may be hard to spot jargon and legalese in your writing. Consider asking someone outside the industry to check your work for incomprehensible words.

Choose the Simpler Synonym

Surround complex ideas with short, common words. For example, use *end* instead of *terminate, explain* rather than *elucidate,* and *use* instead of *utilise.* When a shorter, simpler synonym exists, use it.

Keep the Subject, Verb, and Object close Together

Short, simple sentences enhance the effectiveness of short, common words. We've covered a number of guidelines for writing shorter sentences, but there are a few more you can use to streamline your writing further.To be clear, sentences must have a sound structure. Here are a few ways to ensure yours do.

The natural word order of English speakers is *subject-verb-object.* Your sentences will be clearer if you follow this order as closely as possible. In disclosure documents, this order is frequently interrupted by modifiers.

Write using "if-then" Conditionals

Conditional statements are very common in disclosure documents—although they are rarely written that way. That's why the sentence is easier to read.

Here are four rules of thumb to help you write conditional statements effectively:

1 *One "if," one "then"* When there is only one *if* and one *then,* starting with the *if* may spare some of your readers from having to read the rest of the sentence. In these cases, the *if* clause defines who or what the "then" clause applies to.

   If you invested in Class A shares, then…

2. *One "if," multiple "then"* When there is only one *if* and more than one *then,* start with the *if* and tabulate the *then.*
3. *Multiple "ifs," one "then"* When there is only one *then* and more than one *if,* start with the *then* and tabulate the *ifs.*
4. *Multiples "ifs" and "then"* When there is more than one *if* and more than one *then,* you'll probably need to break it down into more than one sentence, taking care to specify which *ifs* apply to which *then.* If the information is still unclear, consider presenting the information in a table.

Keep Your Sentence Structure Parallel

A long sentence often fails without a parallel structure. Parallelism simply means ensuring a list or series of items is presented using parallel parts of speech, such as nouns or verbs. All writers, regardless of their degree of expertise, occasionally write unparalleled sentences.

The best way to rid your document of them is to read through it once solely to find these mistakes. Reading your document aloud can make unparalleled constructions easier to spot.

Here's an example from a mutual fund prospectus that lacks parallel structure:

Before: If you want to buy shares in Fund X by mail, fill out and sign the Account Application form, making your check payable to 'The X Fund,' and put your social security or taxpayer identification number on your check.

After: If you want to buy shares in Fund X by mail, fill out and sign the Account Application form, make your check payable to 'The X Fund,' and put your social security or taxpayer identification number on your check.

Here is a more subtle example from another mutual fund prospectus:

Before: We invest the Fund's assets in short-term money market securities to provide you with liquidity, protection of your investment, and high current income.

This sentence is unparalleled because its series is made up of two nouns and an adjective before the third noun. It's also awkward because the verb *provide* is too closely paired with the nominalisation *protection.* One logical revision to the original sentence is to change the noun series to a verb series.

After: We invest in short-term money market securities to provide you with liquidity, to protect your investment, and to generate high current income.

All writers, regardless of their degree of expertise, occasionally write unparalleled sentences. The best way to rid your document of them is to read through it once solely to find these mistakes. Reading your document aloud can make unparalleled constructions easier to spot.

How easy is it to read the following sentence once and understand what it means?

Before: The Senior Notes and the guarantee (the 'Guarantee') of the Senior Notes by Island Holdings will constitute unsecured senior obligations of the Issuer and Island Holdings, respectively.

After: The senior notes are an unsecured senior obligation of the issuer, while the guarantee of the senior notes is an unsecured senior obligation of Island Holdings.

Whenever you use 'respectively,' you force your reader to go back and match up what belongs to what. You may be saving words by using 'respectively,' but your reader has to use more time and read your words twice to understand what you've written.

Designing the Document

A plain English document reflects thoughtful design choices. The right design choices make a document easier to read and its information easier to understand.

Some documents suffer because no one knew how basic design decisions, like type face selection, dramatically determine whether or not a document is easy to read. Other documents suffer because expensive design features give them artistic appeal, but at the cost of obscuring the text. In a plain English document, design serves the goal of communicating the information as clearly as possible.

Check with your in-house printing or graphics department—your company may have already dealt with design issues in other documents or may have skilled designers who can help you with your document.

Since some standards or guidelines in your style manual may have been adopted when plain English was not a concern, review them to ensure they contribute to good design and ease of reading.

If you are using a designer, keep the following in mind:

1. Good design requires clear communication between the writer and the designer. Keep the lines of communication open and flowing.
2. Take the time to explain the nuances of your document to your designer.
3. Don't move into the design phase until your text is final. Once the document is put into page layout software, or once it is at the printer, making text changes can be tedious and expensive.

While the field of design extends broadly, this section covers five basic design elements and how they contribute to creating a plain English document:

1. Hierarchy or distinguishing levels of information
2. Typography
3. Layout
4. Graphics
5. Colour

Hierarchy

Much like an outline, a document's hierarchy shows how you've organised the information and helps the reader to understand the relationship between different levels of information.

A typical hierarchy in the prospectus might include:

a) the document title

b) section headings

c) subsection headings

d) paragraph headings

e) general text

Designers use different type faces in the headings to distinguish these levels for the reader. As a rule of thumb, there should be no more than six levels in the document, excluding the document's title. You can signal a new level by varying the same type face or by using a different type face.

Typography

Although it may seem like a minor decision, your type face selection will be one of the elements that most strongly defines the design and readability of your document.

Kinds of Type faces

Type faces come in two varieties: serif and sans serif.

All serif type faces have small lines at the beginning or ending strokes of each letter. Virtually all newspapers and many magazines use some form of serif type for their general text because serif fonts are easier to read than sans serif. Other popular serif type faces are: Caslon, Century Schoolbook, Garamond, and Times.

Selecting the Right Type face

When choosing a type face, think carefully about where the type face will appear in the document. Some type faces are harder to read than others and were never intended for text. Type faces like Boldine Poster or other bold, italic, or condensed type faces were designed for headlines or for large display type. You can mix different type faces, but do so with discretion; not all type-faces work well together.

Type Measurement

All type faces are measured in points. But don't assume that different type faces in the same point size are of equal size. Also, it is important to choose a legible type size.

Emphasising Text

It's common in disclosure documents to see blocks of text in bold and upper case letters. The capitalisation and bold type attempt to catch the reader's attention. Unfortunately, those capitals make the text difficult to read. Ironically, readers tend to skip sentences written in all upper case.

To highlight information and maintain readability, use a different size or weight of your type face. Try using extra white space, bold type, shading, rules, boxes, or side-bar in the margins to make information stand out. Whatever method you choose to highlight information, use it consistently throughout your document so your readers can recognise how you flag important information.

Layout

Designers think carefully about white space, column width, line spacing, and paragraph length. These design elements determine whether reading is easy or becomes too much of a physical or mental chore.

Effective use of white space

Generous use of white space on the page enhances readability, helps to emphasise important points, and lightens the overall look of the document. White space especially affects the readers of disclosure documents because these documents usually feature dense blocks of impenetrable text.

You should fight the impulse to fill up the entire page with text or graphics. The use of white space between sections or subsections helps readers recognise which information is related.

Use left justified, ragged right text

Research shows that the easiest text to read is left justified, ragged right text. That is, the text is aligned, or flush, on the left with a loose, or ragged, right edge.

Fully justified text means both the right and left edges are flush, or even. When you fully justify text, the spacing between words fluctuates from line to line, causing the eye to stop and constantly readjust to the variable spacing on each line. This, coupled with a severe shortage of white space, makes these documents visually unappealing and difficult to read. Be especially wary of centring text, or using text to form a shape or design. Uneven margins may make a visual impact, but they make reading extremely difficult.

Use line spacing to lighten the page

Line spacing, or "leading refers to the amount of space between lines of text. Leading controls the density and readability of the text. Just as type is measured in points, so is leading. A type description of 12/16 means that 12pt type has been set with 4pts of additional leading between the lines.

Avoid setting type without any additional leading sometimes referred to as being "set solid." Typically, you should allow *at least* 2pts of leading between lines of type. You may want to add more leading, depending on the "airiness" you would like the document to have.

Keep lines to a reasonable ength

A comfortable line length for most readers is 32 to 64 characters. Any longer than that, and your readers will lose their place when they read from line to line. A safe rule to follow is: the smaller the type size, the shorter the line length. Columns also help your readers to move quickly and easily through large amounts of text. An average column width can vary from 25-40 characters.

Keep paragraph short

To reduce dense text, keep paragraphs as short as possible. Even though paragraph length is determined by content, here are some design tips that can help to lighten a long paragraph.Use bullets to list information wherever possible.

Use tables to increase clarity

Use tables to increase clarity and cut down text. Tables often convey information more quickly and clearly than text.

GRAPHICS

Graphics often illuminate information more clearly and quickly than text. The best known work, *The Visual Display of Quantitative Information,* by Edward R. Tufte, provides practical advice on creating graphics. In the introduction of his book, he writes about the importance and value of graphics:

> At their best, graphics are instruments for reasoning about quantitative information. Often the most effective way to describe, explore, and summarise a set of numbers—even a very large set—is to look at pictures of those numbers. Furthermore, of all methods for analysing and communicating statistical information, well-designed data graphics are usually the simplest and at the same time the most powerful.

In his book, Tufte formulates a number of basic principles to follow in creating excellent graphics. Among them are these:

> Graphical excellence is that which gives to the viewer the greatest number of ideas in the shortest time with the least ink in the smallest space.

And graphical excellence requires telling the truth about data.

A few experts have studied the use of graphics in securities documents, isolating the areas presenting the most problems. We can boil down their advice to these guidelines.

Keeping the Design Simple

Keep the design of any graphic as simple as possible. Pare away any nonessential design elements so the data stands out. Think of it this way: as much of the ink as possible in a graphic should deal with a data point and not decoration.

Check Proportions of Visuals

Generally, you should avoid graphics that start at a non-zero baseline, because they distort differences by destroying correct proportions.

Draw Graphics to Scale

Any graphic should be proportionately correct or drawn to scale.

Be Consistent when Grouping Graphics

If you group graphics side-by-side, avoid changing your scale from one graphic to another, as in the examples above.

Don't Reverse Time

In graphics showing information over time, should flow forward, not backward. In these examples, even though the first graphic is clearly labelled, it gives a false visual impression that earnings are going down over time rather than up.

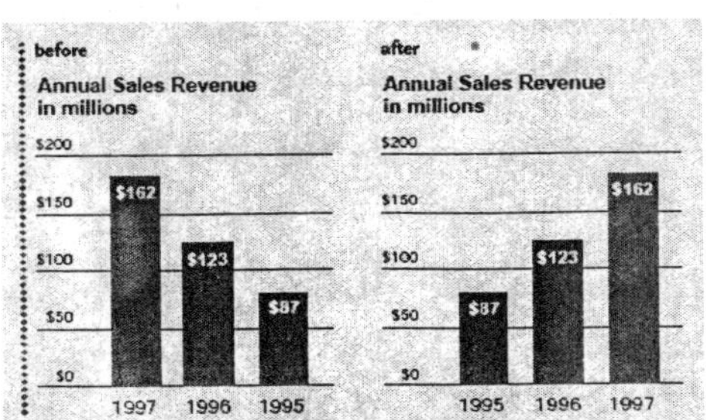

Organise Data to Hasten Insights

Choose an organisation that helps the reader grasp information and comparisons quickly. For instance, if you have a list of foreign stock markets showing their returns in one year, list them in descending order by the magnitude of their returns instead of in alphabetical order.

Integrate text with Graphics

A graphic and its text should be together. You don't want to break your reader's concentration by separating the two, forcing your reader on a detour to another page in search of the graphic that goes with the text.

Don't Use pie charts

According to Tufte, "...the only worse design than a pie chart is several of them....". Most readers find it difficult to draw accurate comparisons between pie slices or between multiple pie charts because the slices form irregular shapes. Showing the same information in a table can often be clearer.

Don't forget your Typography

When choosing a type face for text such as axis labels, consider using a sans serif type face if the type is small and the text is short in length. If you want to insert a note or explanation directly on the graphic, use a serif font if the text is long.

Trust your eye

Finally, one guideline rises above all others in importance and rests squarely with you. Cultivate an appreciation of graphics and then trust your eye. If a graphic seems unclear or unhelpful to you, no matter how many "guidelines" it follows, it probably is.

2

Developing Writing Skills

Learning how to write a coherent, effective text is a difficult and protracted achievement of cognitive development that contrasts sharply with the acquisition of speech. By the age of 5, spoken language is normally highly developed with a working vocabulary of several thousand words and an ability to comprehend and produce grammatical sentences. Although the specific contribution of a genetic predisposition for language learning is unsettled, it is apparent that speech acquisition is a natural part of early human development.

Writing an extended text at an advanced level involves not just the language system. It poses significant challenges to our cognitive systems for memory and thinking as well. Indeed, writers can put to use virtually everything they have learned and stored away in long-term memory. But they can only do so if their knowledge is accessible, either by rapidly retrieving it from long-term memory or by actively maintaining it in short-term working memory.

Thinking is so closely linked to writing, at least in mature adults, that the two are practically twins. Individuals who write well are seen as substantive thinkers, for example. The composition of extended texts is widely recognised as a form of problem solving. The problem of content—what to say—and the problem of rhetoric-how to say it—consumes the writer's attention and other resources of working memory. Finally, the written text serves as external form of memory that others can read and reflect upon, providing a scaffold for thinking and writing in the historical development of a literate culture.

Learning how to compose an effective extended text, therefore, should be conceived as a task similar to acquiring expertise in related culturally acquired domains. It is not merely an extension of our apparent biological predisposition to acquire spoken language. Rather, it is more similar to learning how to type—which is in fact one aspect of composition, as a common means of motor output. Or, it is similar to learning how to play chess—which is another planning intensive task similar to composition in its demands on thinking and memory. Becoming an expert typist, chess player, or, say, violinist, requires a minimum of 10 years of intensive learning and strong motivation to improve. The very best violinists, for example, have accumulated more than 10,000 hours in solitary practice, whereas lesser experts least accomplished experts and amateurs have devoted proportionally less time to self-improvement.

The theme of this chapter is that learning to become an accomplished writer is parallel to becoming an expert in other complex cognitive domains. It appears to require more than two decades of maturation, instruction, and training. The central goal is to gain executive control over cognitive processes so that one can respond adaptive to the specific needs of the task at hand, just as a concert violinist or grand master in chess must do. Accordingly, we should look to the principles of cognitive apprenticeship, with a focus on deliberate practice, in developing interventions that train as well as instruct writers.

We know that many different types of knowledge related to text content and discourse structure must be available in long-term memory. We know that instruction across disciplines and writing instruction in particular must necessarily impart such knowledge. The focus here is on the equal imperative to train writers so that they can retrieve and use what they know during composition, as dictated by the knowledge-use principle.

Development of Writing Skills

The development of written composition skills are conceived here as progressing through three stages, as illustrated in Figure 1. It takes at least two decades of maturation, instruction, and training to advance from (1) the beginner's stage of using writing to tell what one knows, to (2) the intermediate stage of transforming what one knows for the author's benefit, and to (3) the final stage of crafting what one knows for the reader's benefit. The first two stages are well-established by developmental research and typically mastered by advanced high school and college students. The third is seldom discussed, perhaps because it characterises only mature adults who aim to become skilled professional writers.

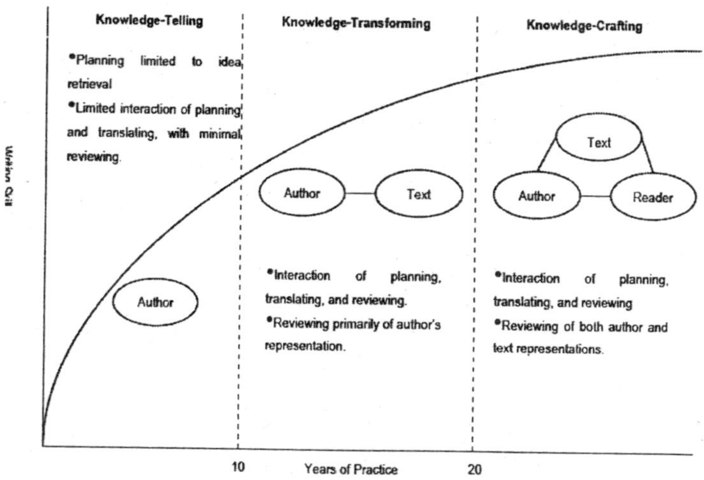

Figure 1. Macro-stages in the cognitive development of writing skill

The three stages are intended to demarcate three macro-stages of writing development. Writing skill is shown as continuously improving as a function of practice, as is typical for perceptual-motor and cognitive skills in general. The micro-changes underlying the gradual improvement that drive the transition to the next macro-stage fall beyond the scope of the present article. As a consequence of the task specificality, a child might be operating at a more advanced stage in writing, say, narrative texts, assuming these are most practised, compared with persuasive texts.

AUTHOR, TEXT, AND READER REPRESENTATIONS

In the most advanced stage of knowledge-crafting, the writer is able to hold in mind the author's ideas, the words of the text itself, and the imagined reader's interpretation of the text. The representations of the author, the text, and the reader must be held in the storage components of working memory and kept active by allocating attention to them. Thus, for expert writers, not only are the basic processes of planning, sentence generation, and reviewing juggled successfully, but so are three alternative representations of content.

By contrast, during earlier stages of a writer's development, the text and reader representations may be either relatively impoverished or sufficiently detailed but not adequately maintained in working memory during text composition. A young child of, say, 6 years of age might have a only partial representation of how the text actually reads in comparison to a much richer representation of his or her own ideas. Gradual gains in writing skill within the stage of knowledge-telling across several years of writing experience would stem from growth in the child's ability to represent the text's literal meaning. Similarly, a 12 year old might be aware of the prospective reader, but this reader representation may be too unstable to hold in working memory.

The stage of knowledge-telling is dominated by the author's representation. By the stage of knowledge-transforming, the text representation is both sufficiently detailed and stable enough to maintain in working memory to permit an interaction between the author and text representations. Yet, the reader representation is not yet routinely entered into the interaction in working memory until the stage of knowledge-crafting. It must first become sufficiently elaborate and stable to maintain *and* working memory resources must be available to coordinate all three representations.

Knowledge-telling

The initial stage of knowledge-telling consists of creating or retrieving what the author wants to say and then generating a text to say it. The author is not entirely egocentric in knowledge-telling and can begin to take into account the reader's needs. Specifically, by the time children are beginning to write they realise that another person's thoughts about the world may differ from their own. By about the age of 4, children have acquired a theory of mind that allows them to take another's perspective. This helps them to plan what they need to say or write to communicate their ideas.

However, it would appear that the writer's representation of what the text actually says to him or her and, to an even greater degree, how the prospective reader would interpret the text as written are impoverished early on in writing acquisition. As the child develops during middle childhood and adolescence, first the text representation, and then the reader representation, gradually become richer and more useful to the composer. The assumption made here is that the author must first be able to comprehend what the text actually says at a given point in the composition before he or she can imagine how the text would read to another person. It is further assumed that these representations must be constructed by the writer in a stable form before he or she can hold these representations in working memory and make use of them in planning and reviewing.

What is known empirically is that writers operating at the initial knowledge-telling stage of development clearly struggle with understanding what the text actually says. As Beal observed, young writers who compose by telling their knowledge have trouble seeing the literal meaning of their texts, as those texts would appear to prospective readers. The verbal protocol collected by Barretor and Scardamalia of children clearly document the essential focus on the author's representation rather than the text and reader representations. The text produced is essentially a restatement of their thoughts.

Knowledge-transforming

The second stage of knowledge-transforming involves changing what the author wants to say as a result of generating the text. It implies an interaction between the author's representation of ideas and the text representation itself. What the author says feeds back on what the author knows in a way not observed in knowledge-telling. Reviewing the text or even ideas still in the writer's mind can trigger additional planning and additional language generation. In reading the text, the author builds a representation of what it actually says. At times such reviewing may lead to a state of dissonance between what the text says and what the author actually meant, but it can also become an occasion for rethinking afresh the author's ideas. During knowledge-transforming, the act of writing becomes a way of actively constituting knowledge representations in long-term memory. The text actually produced is a greatly condensed version of the author's thought processes. When the transition to knowledge-transforming is completed, it is clear that the writer can maintain and use both the both the author and text representations.

Knowledge-crafting

The third stage characterises the progression to professional expertise in writing. The writer must maintain and manipulate in working memory a representation of the text that might be constructed by an imagined reader as well as the author and text representations. Notice that this stage now involves modelling not just the reader's view of the writer's message but also the reader's interpretation of the text itself. In knowledge-crafting, the writer shapes what to say and how to say it with the potential reader fully in mind. The writer tries to anticipate different ways that the reader might interpret the text and takes these into account in revising it. As Summers observed in journalists, editors, and academics, "experienced adult writers imagine a reader whose existence and whose expectations influence their revision process."

Holliway and MC. Cutchen stressed that the coordination of the author, text, and reader representations "builds on multiple sources of interpersonal, cognitive, and textual competencies" and may well account for most of the difficulties that children experience with revision. In an early study of expert versus novice differences in writers, Summers documented that professional writers routinely and spontaneously revise their texts extensively and globally, making deep structural changes. They express concern for the "form or shape of their argument" as well as "a concern for their readership". By contrast, college freshmen made changes primarily in the vocabulary used to express their thoughts. Lexical substitutions predominated rather than semantic changes. There seemed to be little interaction between the text and author representation in her sample of college freshmen, let alone a focus on a reader representation.

It is too strong a statement to suggest that adolescents and young adults always fail to make changes in meaning or take into account the needs of the reader as they review. For example, Myhill and Johne's reported that students aged 14 to 16 can verbalise such concerns when prompted to comment on their writing processes after a writing session. As many as half of their sample of 34 students commented on revisions made to improve coherence and add text in addition to avoiding repetition and making it sound better in general. It is suggested, though, that working memory limitations in holding and manipulating representations of how the reader interprets the text, while simultaneously managing the author and text representations, is a fundamental brake on the writing skill of developing writers throughout childhood, adolescence, and young adulthood.

Tellingly, college students benefit by simply providing them with 8 minutes of instruction to revise globally before they are asked to start a second and final draft of a text. Although this could be interpreted to mean that the students lack the knowledge that revision entails more than local changes, the results of Myhill and Johne's with 13-14 year old render such an interpretation unlikely. An alternative interpretation is that, when left to their own devices, college students invest their available working memory resources as best they can, but still fail to maintain the reader representation needed in making deep structural changes to the text. But they typically do not do so in their college writing assignments to avoid short-changing the time and effort devoted to other necessary processes and representations during composition and subsequent revision.

Finally, interventions that prompt the writer to "read-as-the-reader" explicitly focus working memory resources on the reader representation. These are effective in improving the revising activities of 5th and 9th graders as well as of college students. However, it is unclear from these studies what costs are incurred when limited attention and storage capabilities are focused on the reader representation rather than on the author and text representations. In all of these studies, the task involved writing a text that described a geometric figure to the reader and thus possibly limited the importance of interactions between author and text representations and knowledge-transforming.

To summarise the studies reviewed here and the argument made, even young children understand that they must take into account the reader's thoughts as they compose a message in oral and written communication during the first stage of knowledge-telling. Yet, being aware of a fictional reader in generating text is different from being able to read the text as it is currently written from another person's perspective. Audience awareness should be regarded as a necessary, but not sufficient, condition for eventually developing the capacity to read and interpret the author's own text from the standpoint of an imagined or fictional reader. An additional necessary condition is having a sufficiently developed working memory system to coordinate the author, text, and reader representations concurrently with relative ease. Executive attention, in particular, must be fully mature and effectively deployed to maintain and manipulate all three of these representations as the writer recursively plans, generates, and reviews the emerging text. In knowledge-crafting, the reader's interpretation of the text must feed back to the way the text reads to the author and to the message the author wishes to convey in the first place. Knowledge-crafting, then, is characterised by a three-way interaction among representations held in working memory. By anticipating in detail the responses of readers to an existing text, the writer operating at the level of knowledge-crafting engages in extensive revisions at all levels of the text.

The concept of knowledge-crafting proposed here draws from the work of Walter Hong. About 30 years ago, Hong argued that a skilled author creates a fictional audience for the text to understand its meaning from the prospective readers' point of view. In contrast to oral communication, the audience for written communication is not actual, but fictional, a product of the writer's imagination that can play an active role in composition. As Hong explained, "the writer must anticipate all the different senses in which any statement can be interpreted and correspondingly clarify meaning and to cover it suitably." To effectively interpret the text from the reader's point of view, the author is forced to think about and decide what knowledge the reader already knows that need not be made explicit in the text. Tomlinson underscored the point that mature scholars absolutely must by necessity represent their audience fully because "those who accept or reject or manuscripts, or, worse, those who hire and fire us" are decidedly real rather than fictional readers.

Writing development, then, is not complete at the end of university or even postgraduate work. An individual who writes on the job as a professional, even if it is but a part of his or her work, is preoccupied with what the text says in relation to what the writer already knows. Such domain-specific knowledge may have several beneficial effects for the writer, but one would be the ability to interpret the text as written thus far from the vantage point of another member of the scientific community.

Advanced level, academic writers know their disciplines deeply enough to be able to anticipate their readers' responses to the text they are composing and revising. From examining 240 published research articles from a variety of disciplines and conducting interviews with authors, Hyland identified the ways that readers are drawn into the text. The use of the inclusive we or second person pronouns are one way of binding the reader together with the writer. Another is the use of personal asides that "appeal more to the readers willingness to following their reasoning". A third is to employ directives to readers to see matters as the author desires or, more subtly, "to *note, concede,* or *consider* something in the text, thereby leading them to a particular interpretation"

Even so, it should be noted that even experienced authors vary in the degree to which they explicitly represent their readers in working memory. Christ asked faculty member to inform readers about the writing program that they teach and to persuade the readers as to the value of freshmen composition. They wrote two such texts, with one addressed to incoming freshmen and another to an interdisciplinary faculty committee. Whereas one interpreted both audiences as "skeptical, if not hostile; another expected both audiences to be 'friendly but uninformed' and yet another writer rarely analysed either of the audiences, concentrating instead on exploring her topic in depth".

It is important to remember that the process of reviewing ideas and text is not limited to the revision phase of composition. It is usually embedded in the composition of a first draft, along with planning and language generation. The reviewing of ideas alone—perhaps held solely as mental representations or perhaps recorded as visual-spatial symbols or brief, cryptic verbal notations—an even occur during pre-writing before a first draft is undertaken. Highly extensive reviewing during pre-writing and drafting characterise the strategy of attempting to produce a perfect rather than a rough first draft. Thus, the capacity to see the text from the perspective of the reviewer can be put to use during the composition of a first draft rather than delayed until revising an initial effort, depending on the strategy adopted by the author. Whereas some use a linear strategy of extensive planning during pre-writing before starting a draft, others jump right in with a very rough draft and revise endlessly. Both the specific task and the medium or tool used for writing influence the choice of composing strategies. Regardless of the particular composition strategy employed, what characterises the knowledge-crafting of expert writers is the capacity to keep in mind how a reader would interpret the text as well as representing the author's ideas and what the text says, in its present form, communicates to the author and to the reader.

Rule of Developing Expertise

Studies of outstanding performers in music, chess, type-writing, and other domains indicate that deliberate practice must continue for a minimum of a decade for an individual to acquire expert standing. In the case of composition, the clock starts early, since spoken language and scribbling are developed in proletariate children. By the age of 14-16 years, children have spent 10 years mastering the mechanics of handwriting and spelling, achieving fluency in written as well as spoken production, and mastering the telling of knowledge. Approximately a second decade of practice is needed to advance from knowledge-telling to knowledge-transforming.

It is unknown precisely how long it takes to advance further to knowledge crafting whereby professionals can mentally represent and adeptly process the author's ideas, the text's meaning, and the reader's interpretations of both the author's ideas and the text itself. But several years are probably needed to acquire the domain-specific rhetorical skills and practice at crafting knowledge for a specific audience. Childhood practice at story writing was so commonly mentioned in Henry's ethnographic that "people who were attracted to writing after childhood may even refer to themselves as 'late bloomers'."

Thus, the progression from knowledge telling to knowledge crafting depends on training that must continue from childhood well into adulthood. Even college-educated writers are unlikely to continue the training required to compose like a professional at the level of knowledge crafting.

WORKING MEMORY CONSTRAINS

To summarise, expert writers who have advanced to the stage of knowledge crafting are capable of representing and manipulating three different representations in working memory. They do so by means of complex interactions among planning, generation, and reviewing that must be coordinated through executive attentional control in working memory. Both of these attributes implies a high degree of self-regulation of cognition, emotion, and behaviour that sees the writer through the lonely and challenging job of serious composition.

It is important to understand the heavy demands that are placed on working memory, particularly on the central executive, to see the need for training to free the availability of executive attention for the monitor component of the writing model. One must first reduce the attentional and storage demands of planning ideas, generating text, and reviewing ideas and text for self-regulation to occur. In Beadily's model of working memory, the central executive serves as a supervisory attentional system that controls storage components, such as the phonological loop for verbal representations and the visual-spatial sketch pad for object representations. Verbal working memory maintains representations during the mandatory sub-processes of sentence generation, namely, grammatical, phonological, and orthographic encoding. When concrete nouns are used in a sentence, images of their referents may be stored in the visual-spatial sketch pad. Similarly, spatial working memory appears to have a specific role in generating ideas during planning. Although the phonological loop and visual-spatial sketch pad have a role in writing, it has been argued on theoretical grounds that these storage components are involved in fewer aspects of planning, sentence generating, and reviewing in comparison with the central executive.

In the neuropsychological literature, overall executive functioning is witnessed in planning, reasoning, and emotional regulation tasks that require the coordination of a large number of cognitive processes. Writing researchers have frequently hypothesised and documented the critical role of executive attention in managing the composing process. Interference or slowing in response times to a secondary task measures the degree to which the primary task of writing consumes executive attention. As a person is writing, they respond to an auditory beep that occurs at random intervals. Interference is calculated by subtracting the time needed to respond to the beep when presented in isolation. Writing processes show markedly more slowing in response time compared with other kinds of cognitive tasks.

Rapid concurrent decisions also require executive attention and disrupt writing. Kalsbeek and Sykes found that the need to make decisions about whether to depress a pedal with the right foot or left foot degraded concurrent writing ability. The participant was told to write something interesting, which was possible only when the primary distracting task was slow and easy to perform. Then, only a single word could be written repeatedly and, finally, only a single letter.

Another way to study the issue is to distract executive attention with a demanding primary task, such as holding six digits in mind. Experiments with this and similar kinds of concurrent primary tasks show that when executive attention is drawn away from sentence generation, there is a reduction in sentence length a disruption in grammatical encoding and a slowing in word production.

Given these findings with adult writers, it should not be surprising that the availability of executive attention ought to be a major constraint on the development of writing skill. In fact, Vanden brig and Swanson reported that individual differences in writing ability among high school students are reliably related to central executive capacity.

Writing development, then, seems to echo other important cognitive skills in its dependence on executive functioning. Neo-Piagetian theorists proposed that the limited capacity of a central, domain-independent pool of cognitive resources acts as a brake on progression from one stage of development to the next. The rapid emergence of executive strategies in memory and problem solving tasks similarly depends on the growth of centralised attentional resources. Increased executive control appears to be fundamental to the brain changes that occur during the second decade of life, when concrete thought gives way to the abstract thought of formal operations. Having sufficient executive control over planning, generation and reviewing is plausibly necessary for the production of coherent text. In fact, Scient found that the later transition between concrete and formal operations was associated with the emergence of the ability to generate cohesive links in written texts.

It is also well-established that the basic mechanical skills of handwriting and spelling deplete the limited resources of working memory in children, constraining their ability to generate language fluently. The primary grades of school is the normal period of time for learning the mechanics of writing to a point of automaticity, thus freeing working memory resources for higher order processes. Unless children develop sufficient fluency in handwriting before the age of 12 or so, then their subsequent development of writing skill is weakened substantially.

MC. Cutchen reviewed a wide range of evidence demonstrating that planning, generating, and reviewing are each constrained by the limits of working memory in younger compared with older children. Individual differences in writing ability at a given age are also predicted by differences in working memory capacity. Finally, the self-regulation of planning, translating, and reviewing requires mastery of handwriting and spelling.

To summarise, interactions among planning, generating, and reviewing observed in advanced writers requires available capacity in working memory in several ways. The writer must hold in mind a representation of what he or she wants to say and a representation of what the text actually says. This requires not only well-developed short-term storage capacity, but also executive attention to keep the representations active and to inhibit irrelevant information. Moreover, executive attention must be allocated to coordinating and monitoring the transitions from one basic writing process to the next.

Implications for Writing Education

The implications of these ideas for writing education will be briefly considered next. Educational research has carefully documented the extensive range of knowledge that must be available in long-term memory for effective text composition. A large mental lexicon, heightened grammatical competence, a variety of discourse structures, and domain-specific knowledge of the topic are among these. Accessibility in working memory or through rapid, well-timed retrieval from long-term memory is necessary or else the writer's knowledge is inert during composition.

An expert, professional writer operating at the stage of knowledge-crafting is able to maintain and manipulate in working memory representations of the author's ideas, the text itself, and the prospective reader's interpretation of the text. Both knowledge-crafting and the intermediate stage of knowledge-transforming require the ability to coordinate complex interactions of planning ideas, text generation, and reviewing ideas and text. The most important constraint on developing from knowledge-telling to knowledge-transforming, and possibly then on to knowledge-crafting is the limitations of the central executive component of working memory. It is not enough to know how to plan or how to write clear sentences, for example, if the developing writer is unable to interweave planning and generation in a manner characteristic of mature writers. These basic composing processes must be controlled effectively as well.

In what ways can the educational process aid the functioning of working memory in the service of writing skills? There are undoubtedly numerous ways, but here three points are emphasised. The required degree of cognitive control in working memory of processes and representations most likely depends on (1) maturation of the executive component of working memory, (2) reducing the load on working memory by providing rapid, effortless access to domain-specific knowledge in long-term memory, and (3) reducing the working memory cost of planning, sentence generation, and reviewing processes so that executive attention can be devoted to managing their deployment.

The frontal lobe regions of the brain that support executive functioning mature slowly throughout the decades involved in writing acquisition. High-resolution structural magnetic resonance images reveal a higher degree of frontal development in young adults, 23-30 years of age, compared with 12-16 -year old. These regions quite possibly are needed (1) to maintain simultaneous representations of the author's ideas, the text as written, and the perspective of an imagined reader and (2) to coordinate interactions among planning, generating, and reviewing.

Long-Term Working Memory

Gaining domain-specific expertise allows the writer to retrieve relevant knowledge from long-term memory at just the right moment. Ericsson and Kintsch called this form of knowledge accessibility long-term working memory and distinguished it from laboriously maintaining information in an active state in short-term working memory. This indirectly helps with the overload on the central executive component of working memory by reducing the occasions on which it is needed. The ability to rely on long-term working memory ought to significantly help writers to manage the composition process. Indeed, a high degree of domain-specific knowledge about the topic significantly reduces the momentary demands made on executive attention.

Writing about topics that students know well provides a scaffold to support the writers and to allow them to devote a higher degree of executive attention to the juggling of planning, generating, and reviewing. The writing across the curriculum movement has stressed the value of situating writing assignments within the discourse community of a discipline on the grounds that writing is inherently a social act. While this is certainly true, writing within the discipline of one's major field has the added benefit of allowing the writer to free short-term working memory for the task by relying to some extent on long-term working memory.

Relative Automaticity

Another approach is to directly reduce the demands on the central executive by training the writer in planning, sentence generating, and reviewing skills. There are likely to be multiple ways in which this objective can be achieved and what follows are but a few illustrations.

For example, one can train writers to use strategies that focus effort on a single process at a given moment in time. Preparing an outline during pre-writing helps writers to focus on text generation in producing a first draft. There is still an interaction among planning, generation, and reviewing after outlining first, but relatively more time is devoted to the generating sentences and cohesive links among them when the macrostructure of the text has been sketched out in the form of a hierarchical structure.

Gibberish and Toerance replicated and extended these earlier findings by showing that organised notes aid writing regardless of whether or not these notes are available in preparing a final draft of the text. Just generating text without any planning in advance can also benefit a writer, as long as these initial unorganised notes or sentences are not available to the writer in preparing a final draft. In this case writers use language generation as a planning device When the unorganised notes or sentences are in front of them during final draft composition, writers perhaps divide their attention among planning, text generation, and reviewing. By withdrawing these materials, they perhaps focus more on planning and text generation with less effort given to reviewing what had been produced earlier.

Similarly, it is possible to prompt revisions even in young students operating at the first stage of knowledge-telling. Candour reported that 3rd, 4th, and 5th grade students increase the amount and depth of their revisions when reviewing is delayed rather than immediate. These young writers appear to be capable of correcting ambiguities in texts written by others, but nevertheless fail to do so when writing their own texts and left to their own devices.

In L2 writers 13-14 years of age, Lindgren and Sullivan also found that multiple writing opportunities and post-composition recall of their own writing processes, prompted by a computer-based replay of their keystrokes, enhanced conceptual as well as surface level revisions. Success with such scaffolds for revision in L2 writers certainly indicates their potential value in developing L1 writers as well. Establishing exactly what they strategies are, for whom, and under what circumstances is an important goal for composition research.

One can also train writers so that planning, generation, and reviewing each become relatively automatic. McCutchen made the important point that these processes are too complex to become automatic in the strict sense of becoming effortless, unintentional, and unavailable to conscious awareness. Still, it is certainly possible to reduce the *relative effort* required to plan ideas and their organisational structure, fluently generate sentences and cohesive links among them, and review the plans and text from the perspective of both the author and the imagined reader. In fact, the development of effective writing skill is impossible without reducing these relative demands, according to the argument advanced here. Increased automaticity has been conceived in terms of converting declarative knowledge into procedural knowledge or into retrieval from long-term memory as opposed to computation in working memory. Practice is the means for doing so under either of these models. The best documented cases with respect to writing skill are the relative automatisation of transcription as writers master handwriting and spelling and the revision of subject-verb agreement errors that progresses from a slow, effort full algorithm to a rapid automatic check.

Training Methods

If we think training a writer, much like a musician or an athlete is trained, then what interventions are likely to be successful? One is the tried and true method of learning by doing. That practice makes perfect is so well known as to be a cliche, but the concept of deliberate practice is far more interesting and not well understood in the context of writing. The second method would appear to be the opposite of learning by doing, namely, learning by observing. A cognitive apprenticeship in writing, then, underscores the value of observing rather than doing. Yet, both observing and doing are essential to the learning of complex skills and the two traditions, in good measure, blend well in effective training.

Deliberate Practice

A central factor in the development of expert performance across a wide range of both physical and cognitive task domains is the use of deliberate practice. This method of skill development involves (1) effort full exertion to improve performance, (2) intrinsic motivation to engage in the task, (3) practice tasks that are within reach of the individual's current level of ability, (4) feedback that provides knowledge of results, and (5) high levels of repetition.

Distinguished novelists, for example, credit their success to the use of deliberate practice. In the words of Joys Carol Oates: "I consciously trained myself by writing novel after novel and always throwing them out when completed". Norman Mailer said: " I learned to write by writing. As I once calculated, I must have written more than a half a million words before I came to the *Naked and the Dead.* "

The effects of deliberate practice can be seen in the cumulative productive of authors. As decades of practice take effect, the writer's productivity gains in a non-linear fashion.

Practice can markedly improve college student writing when it is done in the context of a professionally relevant task domain that motivates efforts to learn. John stone, Ash baugh, and War field found that superior writing skills correlated reliably with the degree of repeated practice and, controlling for practice, with writing in the professionally relevant domain of greatest interest to the student. Accounting students who took business writing intensive two courses in their junior year and two more in their senior year gained significantly in their writing skills in comparison with an assessment taken at the end of their second year as sulpho mores. The writing assignments in the treatment group were designed to challenge the students by requiring that they write as accounting professionals for a professional audience. The feedback that students received was consistent and thorough, including grading of grammatical conventions, organisation, professionalism of presentation, technical accuracy of the accounting, and the quality of the analysis.

Learning by doing sounds simple enough, but writing educators need to be aware of the pitfalls in deliberate practice. For example, spaced rather than massed practice is important for two reasons. A common mistake of developing writers is to compose in marathon sessions or binges of massed practice that can exhaust and frustrate the writer. Writing apprehension and even writer's block can result from this misconceived kind of practice at the task. Professional writers learn to compose for just a few hours per day at most, but on a highly consistent daily schedule and students should be trained in the same fashion.

Another advantage of spaced practice is that it maximises long-term learning at the expense of immediate training performance. Although high levels of training performance can be obtained with mass practice, the learning does not transfer as effectively to a different task in the future in comparison with spaced practice. Consider the familiar practice regimen used to teach young children handwriting skills. If instead the child practices a randomly chosen letter on each trial, then training performance suffers some, but transfer tests given

20 minutes or 24 hours after training reveal a clear advantage for the random, spaced practice.

Providing individually tailored feedback is a timely manner is another serious problem in designing effective writing practice. Even holistic grading in the absence of corrections and commentary can be highly labour intensive and subject to poor reliability in large classroom settings. Feedback from an instructor to a student is often measured in days and even weeks rather than minutes and hours. Recent advances in cognitive science and computational linguistics offer the intriguing possibility of automated essay scoring to provide reliable, immediate, and individualised feedback. The commercially available systems called *e-ratter* and *Intelligent Essay Assessor* are two examples. Thus far, however, writing educators have not embraced these systems as even aids to instructors trying to provide effective feedback to developing writers.

Cognitive Apprenticeship

As noted at the outset, there is nothing natural about learning to read and write in the way that learning to speak is part and parcel of normal cognitive development. The acquisition of cultural practices, such as writing, benefits from a cognitive apprenticeship approach in which a mentor provides a model for social learning. Cognitive apprenticeship entails the following features. It involves the learner in guided participation whereby a mentor or coach helps the novice to work through the task at hand. A second core feature is Vygotsky's concept of the zone of proximal development, which focuses learners on tasks that stretch their current capacities so as to reach for growth. By working under a mentor's guidance, the learner is able to perform at a higher level than would be possible when working alone. The best learning tasks, then, are those that lie within the zone of proximal development. Finally, cognitive apprenticeship features learning by observing instead of learning by doing. Apprenticeship underscores the centrality of social learning by observation of the mentor.

Learning by observation has a unique advantage from the point of view that writing overloads executive attention. In observing a mentor, the student can focus attention on the model's behaviour instead of attending to the cognitive processes and motor execution needed to do the task. The best intervention came from observing readers who responded to one's own written text plus receiving additional written feedback.

One final illustration makes clear that deliberate practice and cognitive apprenticeship can be readily integrated in writer training. Skunk & Zimmerman formulated a four step training regimen with the explicit goal of fostering self-regulation. Next, the learner tries to emulate the behaviour of the model. Third, the learner deliberately practices in order to reduce the momentary demands of the cognitive processes underlying performance. Through this reduction, executive attention becomes free to control cognitive processes. Finally, with additional practice at adapting performance to changes in internal and external conditions the self-regulation characteristic of expert performance is achieved.

The point to be made here is that learning by observing can be combined effectively with learning by doing at a different step of the training regimen. The writing intervention data from Zimmerman & Kickstands show that observational learning from a model can produce large effect sizes.

A recent meta-analysis of writing instruction for adolescents supports the tenets of cognitive apprenticeship. Two forms of scaffolding resulted in large effect sizes: peer assistance and mentor assigned goals for the writing project. Different ways of explicitly and systematically teaching students strategies for planning, revising, and editing text so that students can eventually use them on their own also produced large effect sizes. Mastering these techniques through explicit instruction and practice contrasts with simply engaging students in, say, pre-writing activities, which had only a modest beneficia.

Some results of an earlier meta-analysis also can be interpreted as supportive of a cognitive apprenticeship approach. Hillocks found that the most effective interventions assigned well-structured writing tasks with clear objectives, actively guided students in how to solve content and rhetorical problems, and provided peer feedback. These practice-oriented approaches to learning were four times as effective as the Presentation Mode of listening to lectures about how to write.

Two Paradoxes

In light of the arguments raised here, there are two facts about writing development across the life-span that would appear to be paradoxical. The development of writing skills arguably requires decades of learning and moves through increasingly sophisticated stages of knowledge-telling, knowledge-transforming, and knowledge-crafting. Serious written composition simultaneously challenges the human capacities for language, memory, and thinking. The most advanced stage involves routinely and adeptly juggling multiple representations in working memory and coordinating numerous interactions among multiple writing processes.

Both knowledge-transforming and, especially, knowledge-crafting place a heavy demand on working memory resources. In particular, executive attention must be available for self-regulation and this presumably cannot happen without adequate maturation, domain-specific learning, and training. Moreover, as working memory begins to decline with advanced age in older adults, one might equally expect a deterioration of writing ability.

The first paradox, then, is literary precocity in the form of advanced writing skill in very young children, who would appear to lack not only sufficient maturation but also a high degree of domain-specific learning and decades of practising writing to lessen the burden on working memory. Yet, Edmunds and Noel documented a case of literary precocity in Geoffrey, a five year old prolific writer. In their view, Geoffrey had achieved the stage of knowledge-transforming in that he could take source information and work with it so as to yield novel connections and a novel story. Of interest, Geoffrey learned to type at a very young age and showed early mastery of the mechanics of writing, freeing executive attention for higher level processes and a precocious rate of development as a writer. But did Geoffrey really show knowledge-transforming at age five?

A possible resolution of this case with the theoretical argument raised here is that Geoffrey's text revealed no editing at all. Unlike knowledge-transforming, there was no evidence of a preoccupation with trying to modify the text to express the author's ideas more accurately. A second point of resolution is to take note that precocity in writing is extremely rare. Of course, precocious mathematicians, musicians, and chess players are also atypical, but they are far more prevalent than precocious writers, possibly because cultures support very early cognitive apprenticeships in these other domains more commonly than in writing.

The second paradox is that older professional writers are fully capable of composing at high levels of skill despite that their short-term working memory system is likely in decline. It is well established that working memory and executive functioning, in particular, reach their maximum by the third decade of life and noticeably fall off by the fifth or sixth decade. The working memory index of the WAIS-III, for example, drops substantially after the age of 45-54, along with an even steeper decline in the index of processing speed. How is it possible, then, for professional writers to continue as highly effective composers of text well into their 60s, 70s, and even 80s? A second answer may be that older writers come to rely more on retrieval from long-term working memory, lessening the demands placed on the declining functioning of short-term working memory in the first place. Consistent with this view, crystallised intelligence, including verbal comprehension, would appear to depend on retrieval from long-term memory and it remains stable across the life span.

3

Effective Writing Tips

Effective writing generally transmits a clear, concise message that is easily understood, well organised and to the point. Most audiences will understand what message you are trying to convey without difficulty of interpretation.

General Writing Tips

A Write because you have to. If you can accomplish your purpose with a phone call or face to face, do so. Otherwise, make sure you statc the facts briefly and to the point.

B. Make sure you have a clear, defined purpose for your writing. You will have three critical tasks in writing:

(i) to inform or direct.

(ii) to persuade.

(iii) to assess the writing of others.

C. Write so the average reader understands. Tell the audience what they need to know and why. Your main goal is to communicate accurately.

D. Write not to impress but to express your ideas.

E. Write the way you speak. Be personal and don't hide behind the bureaucratic mask. If you write for someone try to adopt his/her voice or tone. Substitute short words for long ones.

(i) Weak words: initiate, terminate, utilise, optimal

(ii) Better: start, end, use, best.

F. Use short, conversational words. Words with three or more syllables are usually cumbersome and misunderstood. Avoid jargon, technical terms and legalism. Jargon is defined as the technical terminology or characteristic idiom of specialists or workers in a particular activity or area of knowledge; often pretentious or unnecessarily vague and obscure terminology. When writing, the use of jargon is often unavoidable; however, those terms can be easily identified by a brief explanation.

(i) Weak: Attached herewith is the report.

(ii) Better: Here is the report.

G. Don't waste your reader's time. Write short sentences, usually 15-20 words, and limit paragraphs to four or five sentences.

(i) Weak: Long sentences often obscure the meaning of the writer and shouldn't be used if clarity is the intention.

(ii) Better: Use short sentences to improve clarity.

H. State your main message in the first sentence. Discuss the detail in the sentences to follow. Make sure your reader knows what your writing is about. Next follow with your purpose, discussion, and conclusions.

I. Use active voice and not passive voice. Active voice is most effective because it is more direct; someone or something is responsible for the action, and the action is stated in fewer words.

(i) ACTIVE: Program managers will review all technical documents in final draft.

(i) PASSIVE: All technical documents will be reviewed in final draft by program managers.

J. Use standard punctuation, spelling and grammar. Above all, make sure your writing is neat and legible.

K. Maintain a consistent point of view by continuing to use one subject; and one tense, mood, and voice in verbs. Sudden shifts in any of these elements tend to obscure meaning and make reading difficult.

L. Use personal pronouns.

(i) Weak: The undersigned requests that your office submit the report to this office.

(ii) Better: Please send us the report.

M. Use proper contractions to avoid wordiness. Improper use of contractions can be confusing.

(i) Weak: It is incumbent upon personnel at all echelons to conserve energy.

(ii) Better: It's everybody's job to save energy.

N. Don't be repetition just for the sake of sounding more important. You avoid getting to the point.

(i) Weak: The project's importance and significance.

(ii) Better: The project's importance.

(iii) Weak: Exceptional, exemplary performance.

(iv) Better: Exemplary performance.

O. Avoid starting sentences with "It is," "There is," and "There are."

(i) Weak: It is necessary to prepare the report.

(ii) Better: You must prepare the report.

(iii) Weak: There are two alternatives mentioned in the report.

(iv) Better: The report mentions two alternatives.

P. Avoid "that" and "which." Use "that" when introducing a restrictive clause. Use "which" when referring to things or ideas.

(i) Weak: I think that the change which they want will cost too much.

(ii) Better: I think the change they want will cost too much.

(iii) Weak: We must replace any equipment that is unreliable.

(iv) Better: We must replace any unreliable equipment.

Q. Don't Use Nominally. Nominally are noun forms of verbs. For clearer writing, try to use the verb form of the noun.

(i) Weak: You must make arrangements to see him.

(ii) Better: Arrange to see him.

(iii) Weak: They held a meeting.

(iv) Better: They met.

R. Rely on active verbs in the present tense, and avoid "will," "will be," and "must be."

(i) Weak: All safe will be checked. The duty officer will spin each safe's dial as part of the inspection.

(ii) Better: Check all safe. Spin each safe's dial when you inspect it.

Elements of Communication

There are four elements of communication:

1. Substance—ideas you want to convey.
2. Organisation—arrangements of parts.
3. Style—how well you understand and how quickly you understand.
4. Correctness—free of grammar, mechanics, and usage errors.

Six-step Writing Process

A. Research. Start with mind mapping or brainstorming. This lets the creative part of your brain work before the ordered part puts the ideas together. Capture what you know about your subject.

   1. Mind mapping Process. This helps determine your purpose and narrow down your ideas:
      (i) Write topic.
      (ii) Write down all ideas that come to you about topic.
      (iii) Determine aim or focus of paper.
      (iv) Determine your intended audience.
      (v) Cross out extraneous ideas that do not relate to your purpose or audience.
      (vi) Group remaining ideas.
      (vii) Eliminate any group or idea that does not support your purpose.
      (viii) Assign headings to each group.
      (ix) Prepare an outline.

B. Plan—there are three parts to planning:
   a) Introduction.
   b) Development.
   c) Conclusion.

4. Begin by forming an outline from your mind mapping. Organise the known information into major parts and organise the groups internally.
5. Establish your controlling idea/bottom line. This will help you organise the major groups and check to make sure you have adequate information to support your bottom line:
6. Establishing your bottom line will vary depending on the organisational style you choose to develop your idea. A decision paper will need a bottom line that announces or takes a position on a topic. An information paper will provide facts. The information must serve a purpose, and the bottom line has to be the purpose of the paper. Make sure your bottom is relevant to the purpose of your paper and to your audience. Make sure the content focused on a single ideal; is it clear? Make sure your information adequately supports your bottom line.
7. Make sure you define the major parts of your groups more precisely and focus on each group, one at a time. You will develop subordinate controlling ideas relating to each major part.
8. Select the sequence of parts to be more effective. Choose a developmental style that will support your bottom line.
   (i) Time—chronological order.
   (ii) Space—spatial order.
   (iii) General to Particular—discuss general idea first and then break down into particular example(s).
   (iv) Particular to General—discuss particular example(s) first and then discuss the overall general idea last.
   (v) Comparison/Contrast—discuss all advantages and disadvantages of your choices.
   (vi) Analysis—break down into parts.
   (vii) Cause and Effect—what will the consequences be of an action.
   (viii) Detail/Example—use examples for support of bottom line.

(ix) Definition—explain an abstract concept (not a dictionary definition).

9. Check for final consistency between:
   (i) Bottom line and purpose.
   (ii) Bottom line and audience.
   (iii) Bottom line and major parts.
   (iv) Major parts and minor parts.
   (v) Form and Sequence Minor Parts—Need to sequence minor parts in the base to support the major parts.

10. Along each pathway from bottom line to major part to subordinate part, you must have a credibility point. Your reader must see the relevance of this point and how it supports your bottom line.

C. *Outline.* You have your plan for how you want to proceed with your paper, you have a bottom line and you have your major parts. Now you must organise these parts into an outline. You are still developing and refining your ideas at this stage.

D. *Draft.* Just start writing everything you have to say. Focus on substance and organisation. Draft Quickly. Don't worry about the perfect work or phrasing; that will slow down your creative process. Use your outline as a road map to keep you on course with your bottom line.
   (i) Choose the best format. Packaging and organising are very important to writing. Certain military papers will require specific formats: Memorandums, Information Papers, Fact Sheets, Decision Papers, Staff Studies, etc.
   (ii) Make your packaging easy to read and follow. The format needs to be easy on the reader's eye. White space is very important in packaging. Use headings, tables, indentions, underlining, highlighting, bold print, capital letters, italic print, colour, columns, etc., in packaging.

E. Revise. This step is difficult especially when you are the author. You are prejudiced because you have an already-present knowledge of what you intend to say. Your drafting stage is much easier because you do not have to worry about style and correctness. In revising, you try to see your material from your reader's point of view. You need to see your material from the perspective of who will read it.

1. Check your substance, organisation, style, and correctness; is your document relevant, focused, and adequately supported.
2. Follow this checklist to make sure substance and organisation go together:
   a. Introduction—states bottom line; sets stage before bottom line; announces the major parts.
   b. Development—bottom line analysed; major parts defined and concise (not too many and not too few); sequence for best effect; major parts properly analysed; evidence detailed and convincing; useful transitions and summaries.
   c. Conclusion—returns to bottom line; summarises major parts.
3. Make sure your style of writing is effective. Work on style before correctness because style can affect the meaning of your work more than correctness errors. Make sure your style of writing follows the basic steps in structure:
   a. Bottom line—purpose of paper.
   b. Unity—reader must be able to see the connection between the information in the body of your work and your bottom line.
   c. Coherence—information must follow an orderly sequence.
   d. Paragraph Coherence—every paragraph should focus on a single, controlling idea.
   e. Sentence Coherence—every sentence should focus on a single, controlling idea.
   f. Emphasis—stressing key parts to stand out or take on special importance allows the reader to grasp ideas in order of importance.
   g. Adequate Development—did you adequately support your bottom line; have you persuaded your reader.

h. Conclusion—go back to bottom line; make sure you have followed your bottom line and all controlling ideas.

F. Proof. You must check and mark your final copy. Always have someone else do the final editing of your work.

4

Keys to College Writing

College courses demand many different kinds of writing that employ a variety of strategies for different audiences. You may be required to write long essays or short answers in response to examination questions. You may be asked to keep a journal, write a lab report, and document the process you use to perform research. These are only some of the many types of writing you may engage in throughout your college career.

College writing, also called academic writing, is assigned to teach you the critical thinking and writing skills needed to communicate in classes and in the workplace. To acquire and practice these skills, you are asked to write many different types of assignments under different circumstances. Sometimes your teacher will assign a topic and define the audience; sometimes you will be called on to define and limit the topic and audience yourself.

For example, you must decide what sources of information you will use, how you will interpret this information, how you will organise your ideas, and what words and strategies you will use to explain your ideas. College writing offers the opportunity for you to learn many different strategies for approaching writing tasks so that you may communicate how much you know and understand about a subject to a particular audience, usually your classmates or your teacher.

The *expository* nature of college writing, with its emphasis on the knowledge you gain in your college courses and through research, makes such writing different from your previous writing and perhaps more challenging. Teachers may expect your essays to contain more research, show more awareness of differing points of view, and even reflect more sophisticated expository techniques, such as argument and persuasion. You will often use the skills you learn in college writing throughout your career.

College vs. Workplace Writing

Just as college writing is specific to your mission as you earn your academic degree, *workplace writing* is specific to the needs of your job. Most of the time, however, the specific format and content of workplace writing have already been established by others. You may use *templates,* or documents already set up with the correct format and subject headings.

One of the major differences between workplace writing and college writing is reflected in the expectations of those who assign the writing. In the workplace, the emphasis is on producing a written product. In college writing, the emphasis is on writing to think, writing to learn, and writing to demonstrate learning. In a college assignment, you may be expected to understand the process of creating a memo, to clearly explain the new policy, and to demonstrate reader-centred writing techniques in writing the memo.

Your workplace writing may also differ from college writing in the number of abstract ideas it contains and in the ways that you as a writer are expected to work with them. In general, workplace writing conveys information and is predetermined in purpose and form, whereas academic writing shows knowledge and understanding of both content and process.

Although the expectations differ, both the workplace and college offer you many opportunities to write to different audiences and to adopt different styles depending on your assignments. As a manager in business and as a college student, for example, you may write letters, memos, performance evaluations, status reports, financial reviews, feasibility studies, proposals, and many other types of documents.

Emphasis on Writing

Writing is an active thinking process, a way to develop new knowledge for yourself. Your teachers will deliberately create various occasions for learning new subject matter through writing. For example, you might be asked to keep a journal, write a financial analysis, present a formal argument, create a mission statement, perform a strategic analysis, or even write your own case study. As you write about your subject you are helping your mind to work. As you write, you are recording how your mind works and stimulating your thoughts and ideas. The written record of your thinking becomes part of your new knowledge.

In addition to creating new knowledge, writing can help you explore and discover problem-solving strategies. As you progress in your academic specialisation, you will be expected to address more complex problems associated with learning new subject matter. For example, you might be asked to address the issue of whether global warming is actually occurring. You could be asked to decide the feasibility of starting a new business in an international setting. Because these issues require more complex reasoning, you will find that "thinking in writing" about these problems facilitates your efforts to find solutions.

Although college writing assignments differ somewhat in emphasis from your workplace writing, the methods and strategies these assignments teach you will be useful in your workplace writing.

Writing Process

When we speak of the writing process, we are speaking of the writer's unconscious and conscious creativity and the process that writing textbooks generally define structurally. This process is often treated as a linear one that, if followed step by step, will lead to a successfully written product. Although some writers may write this way, most devise their own ways of generating ideas and writing, usually from their own experiences of what works for them.

Writing is a way of thinking. In other words, the quality of your writing depends on the quality of the thinking you do about your topic or your assignment.

The whole writing process can be divided into the pre-writing, writing, and rewriting or revising phases. In the *pre-writing* phase, you might try to clarify

— what you want to write about
— how you think and feel about your topic
— how you want to approach your topic
— what other materials and notes you might need
— how to organise these materials
— what kind of audience you are writing for

You plan the content and organisation of your paper or assignment during this first phase. In the *writing* phase, you implement your plan, working out the details and fine-tuning your thoughts. In *rewriting* or revising, you review what you have written and consider how and where your writing can be improved.

Sometimes, these phases are quite distinct and separate, but for most students, they seldom have clear boundaries. They overlap in a recursive fashion rather than fall in place as an orderly sequence of steps, one neatly following from the other. When you work on longer research papers, you will generate ideas, gather information, plan your organisation, and write your draft. You may later go back to revise it.

Understanding that writing is individual and recursive, we can look at the three phases—pre-writing, writing, rewriting—and some strategies you may use to write college assignments.

Pre-writing

The purpose of Pre-writing is to generate an abundance of raw material and notes that will give you some strategies for writing your first draft. For most students, starting a draft too soon, without the results of the Pre-writing phase, leads to poorly constructed writing, often with weak generalities. Pre-writing is not an isolated event, but the way to look ahead to drafting and revising, enabling a piece of writing to grow.

Pre-writing is a systematic thinking process that helps you probe what you will write. Pre-writing techniques help you determine what *rhetorical* approach to take and how to plan for implementing it. Pre-writing planning enables you to explore a topic from different perspectives, engage your imagination and creativity, discover original ideas, and perceive not-so-obvious relationships between and among ideas.

Understanding Your Assignment

Your writing task begins when you receive your writing assignment from your teacher. The first step is to make sure you understand the assignment and what your teacher wants you to do with it. To do this, review the requirements of the assignment. These may be in the form of an assignment sheet or a description of the assignment, or they may be given to you verbally during a class lecture. In any case, to understand your writing project, you should ask and answer the following kinds of questions:

> What type of assignment is this? What is its purpose?
> Who is the audience for this assignment—my teacher, my classmates, or someone else?
> How will I find my content—from my opinion or research?
> When is the assignment due to the teacher, and in what form is it due?
> How will the assignment be evaluated?
> What are my goals in undertaking the assignment?

Answering this last question is important because your answer determines the level of effort you put into the writing project. Not all writing projects warrant the same level of effort. For example, the thesis you write in your final year to satisfy a graduation requirement will probably require more time and attention and stricter adherence to a systematic writing process than a response you may write for a homework assignment. If you are not sure of the importance of individual assignments, ask your teacher.

To help you understand your writing assignment and decide what approach to take to write it, look for key phrases that reveal your teacher's expectations.

Table 1 shows you how to identify these expectations from the directive wording of the assignment. These key phrases are often associated with essay questions, as well as informal and formal papers. As a note, the table is based on Benjamin Bloom's cognitive objectives.

Once you have understood your assignment and decided on what approach to take, you can move on to identifying and targeting your audience.

Table 1. Assignment Wording and Expectations

Assignment uses the following directive wording:

— Define, label, list, name, repeat, order, arrange, memorise

— Describe, indicate, restate, explain, review, summarise, classify

— Apply, illustrate, prepare, solve, use, sketch, operate, practice, calculate

— Analyse, categorise, compare, test, distinguish, examine, contrast

— Arrange, compose, formulate, organise, plan, assemble, construct

— Use supporting examples, cite passages from the text, paraphrase, summarise

— Provide corroborating evidence, reference other works, research, cite examples from case studies

— Appraise, evaluate, conclude, judge, predict, compare, score

When your teacher expects you to do the following:

— Memorise, recall, and present information

— Interpret information in your own words

— Apply knowledge to new situations

— Break down knowledge into parts and show relationships among parts

— Bring together parts of knowledge to form a whole; build relationships for new situations

— Make judgments based on criteria; support, confirm preferences

— Quote or paraphrase to support what you have written

— Use outside research to support your thesis or hypothesis

Targeting Your Audience

No matter what the writing project, you should plan to write to someone—that is, you should target an audience for your writing assignment. Audience analysis is crucial to understanding what should go into each piece of writing. You should consider your audience's needs in your research; your content; the background information you provide; your tone, style, and wording; and the frequency with which you define terminology.

Many students assume that the teacher is the *primary audience* for the writing. Although your teacher may be your audience for an essay, he or she may also expect you to write for your classmates or others in your field of study.

In addition to knowing who your audience is, you need to understand your *purpose* for writing. Writers always have a specific reason for writing, and purpose includes what the author intends to accomplish in the writing and how the author wants the reader to use the information.

Your purpose is not the same as your writing strategy. To *analyse* some concept is not, by itself, very interesting or meaningful. But to analyse a concept to look closely at its various parts so that you may gain new insight into what it means has both strength of purpose and meaning for the reader.

If you are unsure who the target audience is, discuss the issue with your teacher. Also, be aware of key words on your assignment sheet that will help you identify the intended audience.

To develop an *audience profile*, you need specific information about your audience, information about its understanding of and attitude toward your subject. Your teacher may guide you in learning what questions to ask to get the necessary information to profile your audience, or you may develop this list yourself. The following list, although not exhaustive, can help you do that. Be aware that your teacher or your particular writing assignment may require more information about your audience.

— Who is my primary audience?
— What purpose will this writing serve for my readers? How will they use it?
— Is my audience multi-cultural?
— What is my audience's attitude toward and probable reaction to this writing?
— Will readers expect certain patterns of thought in my writing?
— Will they need statistical data to be convinced?

After you determine the nature of your audience and your purpose, you must determine how this information affects your planning and writing decisions. For example, the audience profile will tell you the following:

— how much information to convey
— what kinds and levels of details to include
— what concepts to emphasise

— how much time to spend in research
— what writing strategies to use
— how to organise your information
— what words, tone, and style to use to communicate with your audience

Some students prefer to answer these questions before they begin to write. Other students begin planning the writing and answer these questions later. Actually, this series of planning activities includes Pre-writing activities and perhaps some research. The goal of this phase of the writing process is to determine the scope of your writing project and to prepare to write your first draft.

We will now describe several Pre-writing techniques to help you get started.

Techniques to Get Started

Where do ideas come from? For most writers, writing is *recursive*, even messy. Writers step into the writing process wherever they can get a foothold to begin. How students develop their own writing process usually depends on their learning styles, personalities, and work habits.

Although everyone begins with the assignment, each writer engages the writing process at a different place and gets to the finished product by a somewhat different means—depending on the assignment, purpose, audience, and what the writer already knows about the subject matter. If you are a first-year student with little writing experience, you might start with the Pre-writing questions about audience, purpose, and topic.

Although successful writers follow different paths that enable them to think about their writing, create and frame ideas, and draft and revise their writing, there are enduring and natural ways of apprehending writing.

Writers have used many different techniques to generate ideas and get started. These techniques can even overcome barriers to writing, known as *writer's block.* Writers can use these techniques at any point in their writing, not just at the beginning. When a writer runs out of ideas after a writing project is underway, these techniques can help him or her to get moving again.

Among several widely used techniques for probing a topic and teasing out various ideas for writing, here's the best short set of techniques to fit a variety of thinking styles.

Using Systematic Techniques

Systematic techniques, those that have a preconceived structure, often work well for students who like to observe and reflect on what they observe. These students, who like to analyse and organise, prefer to have their information in neat packages. They tend to like working with details and directions, following instructions, and ordering their information and work habits. No matter what kind of student you are, try these different techniques to see what works to get you started.

Classic Strategies

You may recognise these classic strategies for getting started as ways to develop or organise an essay. Using this strategy, you would thoughtfully answer a few questions using topics you might like to explore. As you write these answers and think about your topic, you can make brief notes. After reviewing your notes, you mark the ideas that seem promising.

Mining Your Intuition

Intuitive techniques are often choices for writers who tend to discover information through concrete experiences and their own feelings. These techniques—brainstorming and webbing and chaining—appeal to students who don't always know where to begin and who are comfortable generating their own ideas and approaches. Some students just work better when they are able to let their imaginations run free and express their idea associations.

Brainstorming

Brainstorming enables a writer to find ideas that may be submerged in the mind, memory, and intuition. It's a form of *free association* in writing to stimulate a chain of ideas, a technique that teaches you how to think in writing. You can brainstorm with others or by yourself. In any case, when you brainstorm, you create a list of ideas and associations to help you think through your topic. In brainstorming:

— *Set a specific time limit.* To begin, set aside a specific amount of time, such as 5 or 10 minutes. As you brainstorm, suspend your critical mind that edits and censors ideas.

— *Use plenty of blank paper*. Use blank sheets of paper or the blank screen on your computer. It's important to have plenty of space in which to write so you don't run out of space before you run out of ideas. Using unusual writing implements, such as crayons or coloured markers, sometimes opens up your creative thinking and stimulates novel ideas. Some writers tape sheets of paper to a wall; others use a white board.

— *Select a word, phrase, or idea.* When you are ready to begin, set your time and write down everything that occurs to you for that word, phrase, or idea. Write your key phrase at the top, in the middle, or even at the end of the sheet. Keep writing. Don't stop; use what you have written for more ideas.

— *Write quickly without stopping.* The ideas will come rapidly, and you should write everything down immediately without judging its worth. When you brainstorm in a group, designate a recorder to do the writing to keep up with the rush of ideas. The important thing here is to maintain this flow of ideas without stopping.

— *When your time is up, take a break from your brainstorming for a few minutes.* When you return to your list, circle the ideas or phrases that interest you or that suggest something you might like to pursue. This preliminary list can give you key phrases, words, and ideas for still another brainstorming session. You can brainstorm until you are satisfied that you have the ideas you want to work with.

— *When your brainstorming session is over, you can then consciously begin analysing and organising your ideas*. Circle the ideas that might be related and that might interest you. Can you organise these into a topic for your writing assignment? You can even try free writing to form some good ideas for your assignment.

An added benefit of brainstorming is that you are bringing your own personal perspective, knowledge, memory, and creativity to your writing assignment. When you work from your own viewpoint, you are more likely to generate original material.

Webbing and Chaining

Webbing and *chaining* are very similar, using the free association of ideas discovered in a visual kind of way. Begin webbing by putting your topic idea in the centre and drawing radiating lines out from it. At the end of each of these lines, or rays, write down all the ideas that occur to you. Brainstorm for a period of time, such as two minutes, and generate several different ideas.

Outlining

Some students use only the outlining technique to get started in their writing. Formal outlining, which often results from organised lists, is a highly analytical technique that assumes the writer knows already the how, what, where, when, why, and who aspects of the topic. For an *outline* to be effective, the writer must also have some ideas about the writing strategy to use for the assignment. Other writers may start with lists of ideas, organised into related topics, and create a general informal outline of the subject matter.

Many writers in the Pre-writing phase use grocery lists of topics, loosely organised into some sequence that seems to make sense.

At some point, you will have to stop generating ideas and answers to questions and begin organising all your notes and raw material. You will have to decide how to order your material and to shape your draft to meet your needs. There is no clear-cut place to stop Pre-writing activities and begin drafting; the Pre-writing, writing, and revising do not follow a strict linear sequence.

If you have tried these techniques to generate ideas and get started, you now have several pages of information for the next step. You have at least one major idea on which to write, an articulated sense of your interest in the topic, an accounting of what you already know, and some ideas for how to find more information. Add to this substantial start your audience analysis, and you are ready to begin drafting.

Exploratory Research

Doing exploratory *research* is included here with the pre-writing techniques because library research often is a way to generate ideas. As you review the literature on a subject or read in a particular area, you may note ideas that will help you get started with the writing.

We also describe research here because of its part in the transition from Pre-writing to writing. If you decide that research is needed, you should begin it before you create the final version of a thesis and write an outline. Often, research provides information that can help you formulate a thesis or controlling idea. Many times, what you learn from course materials is not enough for formulating a controlling idea. You often have to do some research just to be able to articulate an opinion.

For example, in a technology management course, you may learn that the average time for completing an engineering project is two years. To encourage critical analysis, your teacher may offer examples that both prove and dispute this claim. Your writing assignment may be to propose several methods for shortening the average time. You realise that research will be needed, first, to confirm the average development time, and, second, to discover methods for shortening this time.

Thesis Statement and Controlling Idea

After you have begun the research and decided on your subject, the next step in the planning process is to determine your working thesis. A *thesis statement* states the purpose and topic of your writing, and the *controlling idea* indicates the direction and, often, the *writing strategy* you will adopt. Your thesis statement will often be based on your synthesis of the information you have gathered from class, from your experience, and from research. This early in your writing, your thesis statement is really a *working thesis* that you use to begin thinking about your topic. You may revise this thesis many times before you are finished thinking and ready to write your final draft.

Some students struggle with how to write a thesis statement and how to use it in their writing. Your thesis statement may take its shape from different ways of weaving your material and thoughts together.

The first method is simply to restate the assignment in your own words. Restating the assignment often helps you understand it better and gives you a point at which to begin writing. Table 1 can help you with this method and others. Restating enables you to articulate your point of view and write what you know and how you think about your assignment topic.

The next method works when you have researched your topic first. Simply sum up what your research has led you to believe or what you think it means. This method helps you start organising your thoughts as you look to your research to support your thesis.

The third method works for students who like to jump into the writing with only minimal preliminary organising and planning. Think of your topic as a question, and write your assignment as though you are answering it.

If you are a first-year student for whom college writing is a new experience, your thesis statement may be simple. Your teacher may ask you to write a few paragraphs on a simple topic to demonstrate learning in your course work.

The thesis statement for a more formal research writing assignment might resemble the following, written for a research paper for a capstone course in business management. This thesis statement suggests that the writing will be more analytical and that the author will synthesise the results of the analysis.

Reader-centered writing techniques will make your writing clear, concise, and effective.

Breakthrough research is revolu-tionising the treatment for diabetes, a condition that causes nerve damage manifested by blindness, deafness, loss of feeling, and intense pain.

The design of most information systems will require the systems analyst to use the procedural model, the logical model, and the business-oriented mathematical model.

To make a decision about whether to expand business in Japan or in Canada, a company needs to know the economics and business practices of each culture. Disney's failure in France can be attributed to the company's lack of understanding of the French culture, business practices, and politics.

Many writers use a checklist to evaluate the appropriateness of their chosen thesis statement. Sometimes it's a good idea to have someone else read your thesis statement and give you feedback. Your thesis statement is effective if you can answer yes to these questions.

— Did I state the thesis specifically and include only one main idea to discuss?
— Does my thesis statement tell the reader what my writing strategy is and how I will develop my ideas?
— Can I support my thesis with evidence from class readings, research, and experience?

Once you have a working thesis statement, what do you do with it? Your clearly stated thesis should suggest to you some ideas for organising your information, so now may be a good time to discuss outlining.

Outlining What You Will Write

Your *planning outline* will probably be informal at first as you think in writing and organise your thoughts. As with your thesis, you may revise your outline many times before you are ready to draft your paper, as you gain knowledge of your topic and make decisions about how to organise the information for your audience.

Outlining is just another way to organise your ideas and can be used at every stage of the writing process. Outlining, especially in the planning stages, may be informal, a scratch list of points you want to make. Ideas are often simply jotted down in an order that appears to make sense to the writer in thinking about the topic. At a more developed stage, an outline may expand on several aspects of the thesis and controlling idea.

A formal outline, on the other hand, may contain complete sentences that expand the major and minor supporting statements for the clearly delineated thesis statement. How formal and detailed your outline is depends on the demands of the writing task and what kind of writer you are. Outlining can help you plan and manage your writing assignment in several ways:

— It helps you organise information.

— It facilitates sharing information with your peers and your teacher to see if you are on the right track.

— It helps you to think in writing as you are deciding what to say for your first draft.

When you can see all the main information items in your writing project, you can then plan your research and writing schedule.

Writing

Getting From Notes To Your Draft

Every writer's habits and ways of thinking differ. As you begin your first draft, you will find yourself cycling through four basic activities:

1. Interpreting your notes and research materials
2. Organising your ideas
3. Refining your thesis
4. Revising your draft

Start with your working thesis. As your writing flows from the thesis statement with its controlling idea, the subsequent paragraphs provide the information identified in your lists and notes.As you write, you may want to provide concrete examples and support for what you say. If you are writing an essay, the support may be from the course lectures, excerpts from a text you studied, or examples from your experience that substantiate the points you want to make.

A *first draft,* your initial attempt to organise your thoughts in prose writing, is more complete than an outline and elaborates your ideas in complete sentences and paragraphs. From your thesis statement and notes, you should write at least one draft. For now, disregard spelling, punctuation, and grammar, which are writing *mechanics*. In this draft, you want to focus on getting your ideas down in a way that reflects your outline and your proposed plan. Focus on the content. As you write, you will discover ways to improve your content and even your writing plan. You may decide to move, delete, or add sections. As you refine your ideas about your writing project, keep in mind that too many changes will impede your progress; if the change seems worthwhile, however, don't hesitate to change direction.

Feedback

A writer seeks feedback to begin the revising process. Once you have a draft on paper, you can get feedback from others on whether you have met your stated goals and whether what you have written is suitable. A way to get especially valuable feedback is to give your teacher, classmates, or even your work colleagues a checklist of items you particularly want feedback on.

Table 2. Checklist for Feedback on Your Writing Assignments

Planning and Researching

1. Is the thesis statement clear and focused on one major idea?
2. Are the intent and purpose expressed clearly?
3. Is the target audience clearly defined?
4. Does the scope seem appropriate for this writing project?
5. Is sufficient information provided?
6. Does the author of the paper or assignment consider other perspectives or address possible questions?
7. Are facts and opinions explained and supported in convincing detail?

Organising and Drafting

1. Is the controlling idea sufficiently developed?
2. Are the major ideas defined clearly and sequence logically to fit the purpose?
3. Do the minor ideas clearly support the major ideas?
4. Does the introduction clearly set the stage by announcing the thesis and controlling idea?
5. Does the conclusion return to the controlling idea and review the major ideas?

Revising

1. Do the transitions clearly act as verbal signals?
2. Does the author use logical connections and summarise when necessary?
3. Are there mechanical errors the author should correct?
4. Does the format of the paper promote quick, clear understanding?
5. Do the graphics clarify the text?

As you develop as a writer, you will adopt a positive attitude toward feedback and solicit it whenever possible. Three ways of gaining feedback are:

— Requesting your teacher to approve the wording of your thesis and the general direction and tone of the paper you are writing.
— Asking knowledgeable classmates and colleagues to read your writing so that you know how others familiar with your subject will receive it.
— Soliciting feedback from people who are unfamiliar with your work and the subject you are writing about.

Getting feedback is a precursor to revising your draft, which you may do several times. The comments of others and your own assessment of your work can become the basis for your revision.

Being Your Own Critic

it is a challenge for a writer to be a good editor or proofreader of his or her own writing, but these are useful skills to learn. When you move from writing to editing, you need to approach your manuscript with a fresh eye and an objective interest.

Proofreading, which you will do many times, calls for you to compare your original text with the corrected text to catch any changes you missed or made incorrectly.

Editing requires that you perform a more complex check of your work, evaluating its content, organisation, and style. In editing, you review systematically certain features of your writing:

> Content: Is your information complete and appropriate?
>
> Organisation: Did you develop and order your information logically? Did you provide signals and transitions indicating that order?
>
> Style: Are the style and tone consistent? Do the sentences flow effectively? Did you use accurate vocabulary and appropriate diction? Are the mechanics correct?

To begin editing, print a double- or triple-spaced copy of your paper. Take a top-down approach and review the general organisation and content of your writing. Don't focus on sentence-level editing yet. If you need to rearrange the paragraphs and sections, this is the time to do so. To get a clearer look at how your document is organised, write down your headings or use the document map feature of your word processor to view them.

You will need more than one pass through your paper. Once you have the organisation and content the way you like it, you can pay closer attention to the style. Polish your sentences so they flow logically with your ideas. Be sure your paragraphs and sentences are consistent and correct and your vocabulary and diction appropriate. Ensure that the mechanics are clean—no punctuation, spelling, or style convention errors.

A good way to improve your chances of being a good self-critic is to follow a personalised checklist each time you review your own work. You can write it to reflect what you already know about your strengths and weaknesses as a writer, or you can develop a checklist that will work generally for your writing.

Creating a Revision Strategy

In addition to the personal revision checklist, you may want to create a *revision strategy* based on the amount of time you have to revise and what your paper is likely to need. A revision strategy is a systematic process to review and evaluate your writing before you actually begin revising.

For example, if you are expecting to receive comments from *peer reviewers* a week before the paper is due, and you also know that the paper includes many typographical errors and mechanical errors, you may want to correct those while the paper is out for review.

Your revision strategy should be closely linked to the writing schedule for your project. The overall success of your revision effort will depend on how closely you have followed this schedule up to the point where revision can occur. Even when your time is limited, you should always try to leave some time for revision.

The Final Draft

The *final draft* is what you will hand in as the completed paper. If you are writing an examination, the final draft may be your handwritten answers once you have had a chance to read over them quickly and make corrections.

By the time you write the final draft, your writing should look fairly polished. Choppy sentences, poor or nonexistent transitions between paragraphs, grammar and spelling errors, and other characteristics of a first draft should all disappear. In addition, your final draft should incorporate comments you have received as well as changes you want to make based on your own evaluation.

Before you turn in your final draft, you should read what you have written all the way through at least once more. If you find something wrong with your paper at the last minute, attempt to correct it before you hand it in. Check with your teacher before making minor corrections with a black pen on the final paper.

At this point, you can use the following assessment checklist for your final draft. This checklist is briefs than the previous assessment during the drafting phase. You may, however, use either one to your benefit. Here, your evaluation should determine how well your writing assignment achieved its purposes.

Thinking Strategies and Writing Patterns

During your college career, you will write a variety of assignments. Some will be based on your beliefs and opinions; others will require you to report on and evaluate existing research. You may be asked to write any number of business documents, such as proposals, reports, feasibility studies, strategic planning documents, and even lab reports and other scientific research. You may write speeches, advertising and marketing copy, and white papers as assignments. You may even write fiction, such as short stories and poetry. Most certainly during your college career, you will write research papers and be expected to take essay examinations. Whatever you write, you will need strategies to help you apply your critical thinking skills to the writing process. There is no neat crossover between assignments and thinking strategies. In some cases, these strategies will be clear to you, e.g., when you are asked to analyse a problem and propose a solution. In other cases, the assignment will be expressed more abstractly and call for a variety of critical thinking and writing strategies.

Assignments You Will Write

Most college writing consists of assignments tailored to help you think about the subjects you are learning, learn about and explore new subjects, discover what your ideas are, and demonstrate what you have learned. In other words, your assignments are opportunities for you to pose probing questions that your writing will answer. In learning to pose the questions and answer them, you will discover how writing serves as a thinking tool.

Many students think of writing as what they produce after they have thought through the assignment or the question at hand. In general, if they study the material, students don't have much difficulty writing about the content of the courses. By understanding that you can use writing to explore and discover ideas for your assignments, you can generate ideas, discover what you think about your topic, explore approaches to it, and demonstrate critical thinking about it, all of which constitute what your teacher hopes to accomplish in assigning writing tasks.

Assignments usually embody certain learning objectives called cognitive objectives. Just knowing what learning objective is intended for an assignment can head you in the right direction.

In the first three levels of cognitive objectives, you are expected to demonstrate your knowledge and mastery of course information. You show that you remember facts and can recall them comprehend the information by being able to interpret and present it in your own words, and apply what you are learning to new situations (application). The remaining cognitive objectives—analysis, synthesis, and evaluation—are more complex and represent the kinds of learning objectives fostered in the college experience.

Critical Strategies and Writing

The writing process is messy. Experienced writers do not follow a neat set of procedures to achieve their writing goals. They use writing to discover and explore. Asking questions and writing go together; writing is about thinking. Only after the writer thoroughly examines the subject through writing and is satisfied with the ideas discovered, does he or she polish the writing for the reader.

Critical thinking yields several strategies you are likely to use in your college writing. Your writing assignments may primarily reflect just one of the strategies or a combination of them. We have arranged these strategies in the order of complexity of the critical thinking they require. Keep in mind that these strategies often overlap. But you will use several of these analytical strategies when you write an evaluation. You should look at the discussion here as a way to explore and discover your ideas about your subject so that you can write your assignment.

The strategies discussed here are those most commonly used in college writing. The first three— (1) analysing, (2) comparing and contrasting, and (3) explaining causes and effects—are among the most practised forms of analysis. The next two strategies—(1) stating your opinion and supporting it and (2) proposing a solution—are the forms of synthesis most commonly found in college writing. The last strategy, persuasion, is used with the other strategies to lend credibility to your stated position and to bolster acceptance of your thinking.

Analysis

Analysis, the basis of many other strategies, is the process of breaking something into its parts and putting the parts back together so that you can better understand the whole. When you focus on understanding something better by *comparing and contrasting* it to something else, you identify and analyse the similarities and differences. As you discuss these in your writing, keep your working thesis with its controlling idea in mind. When you seek to explain the *causes and effects* of an action, event, or situation, you are trying to identify their origins and understand their results. You may discover a chain of events that explain the causes and effects. How you decide where the boundaries of causal analysis are depends on your thesis and your purpose for writing.

Synthesis

Synthesis is a bit more complex than the analytical strategies just discussed. In synthesising information, you must bring together all your opinions and research in support of your thesis. You integrate the relevant facts, statistics, expert opinion, and whatever can directly be observed with your own opinion and conclusions to persuade your audience that your thesis is correct.

Evaluation

Evaluation is the most complex of all analytical strategies and uses many of the other analytical techniques. In applying this strategy, you first establish the criteria you will use to evaluate your subject, apply them to the specific parts of the subject you are judging, and draw conclusions about whether your subject meets those criteria. In the process of evaluating a subject, you will usually be called upon to render some analysis and synthesis and even use persuasive or argumentative techniques. In communications classes, you may evaluate user manuals, technical reports, or business proposals. In management classes, you may evaluate particular management techniques and their effectiveness in organisations of a certain size.

Persuasion

Persuasion is aimed at changing readers' opinions or beliefs or encouraging them to accept the credibility or possibility of your opinion or belief. At some level, all writing has a persuasive element. You may simply be persuading your reader to continue reading your writing or even to accept in your credibility, that you know your subject area. Or you may be persuading your reader that your complex theory about the causes of the crash of the Asian market are credible and probable.

You can make your writing persuasive by responding to your reader's needs. When you keep your reader in mind, you can identify with his or her point of view and attitudes. Use your style and tone to show respect for your reader. Offer your reader arguments and evidence—the examples, textual allusions, or research.

Whatever critical strategy you use to write your paper, you will be supporting your thesis statement. Indeed, a well-developed thesis statement will often suggest the writing strategy you should use.

Developing a Paper Using Strategies

After you have discovered and explored your ideas by writing and are satisfied with your content, you can begin organising your ideas for your reader. The key to well-organised writing is to use a strong thesis statement that suggests a key writing strategy to guide your organisation. For each strategy, its use, the reasoning that guides it, and the details that support it are described.

This is a good time to review the examples of *thesis statements. By* realising that the thinking strategies overlap, you can see for yourself how different thesis statements might yield different thinking and writing strategies. The strategies you use should always be guided by your purpose and your audience.

Your introduction and conclusion frame your writing and give it a sense of connection and resolution. The introduction establishes your idea and purpose, whereas the conclusion affirms your thesis and resolves your thinking process. For many students, having a clear introduction with its thesis statement and major supporting statements is enough to guide their writing.

With a clear thesis statement to guide you, can write your introduction, one of the key sections of your assignment. Your introduction sets the stage, telling your reader what your thesis is and often what your major supporting statements will be and suggests the strategy for the writing.

Sometimes, just knowing that paragraphs consist of a topic sentence with its controlling idea, details, reasons, and illustrations is enough to get a student writing.

Patterns for Presenting Information

College students face a variety of writing tasks in their course work. Although these tasks vary from course to course and discipline to discipline, the ways to present information are similar.

General-to-Specific Pattern

The general-to-specific pattern is probably one of the more common patterns in college writing. It may be used in any of these familiar places:

introduction to a paper
background in a research paper
opening paragraphs for a discussion or an analysis
essay examination answers

As the name suggests, this pattern is characterised by a movement in your thinking from a generalisation to specific details. Your opening paragraph would begin with a general statement and then add details that explain it. The details may continue to become increasingly more specific. The pattern ends with a broad statement that summarises your thinking that resulted from the details.

In this example, the first sentence presents the general statement about the writing process. The succeeding statements consist of details and examples, introduced by the transitions *first*, *second*, and *third*. Finally, the pattern ends with a broad or general statement that summarises what the writer wishes to conclude about the meaning of the details.

This paragraph could have introduced a longer paper in which the writer discusses the kinds of training needed to learn to write, analyses the results of a study about learning to write, or even introduces a topical literature review about teaching writing.

You might find this pattern useful for writing mission and vision statements, definitions, marketing analyses, reports of scientific investigations, topical literature reviews, feature articles, editorials, and formal arguments from principle. Also, this mode of writing reflects deductive reasoning, where your conclusion follows necessarily from your premises

Specific-to-General Pattern

The specific-to-general pattern reverses the one we just discussed. A paragraph written in this order begins with the details and leads the reader to the generalisation, which may be the thesis or the conclusion.

This pattern is as compelling as the general-to-specific pattern. As you lead the reader through your thinking, you can build some suspense before your concluding statement. Writers often use this pattern to persuade their audience about the writer's generalisation or conclusion and when he or she isn't sure about the audience's attitude toward his or her conclusions.

This pattern is especially useful for writing that seeks to discover the nature of the problem and the possible solutions by carefully analysing their details. For example, in writing a diagnosis of organisational problems, the writer might use *inductive reasoning* to find the major problems by examining the symptoms. These results may be presented in a specific-to-general order.

Problem-Cause-Solution Pattern

The problem and solution pattern reflects a form of critical thinking that tends to be more argumentative and evaluative. You may find this pattern useful in writing case studies, critiques, introductions, reports of scientific investigations, literary reviews, political and social discourse, white papers, proposals, many kinds of reports, and essay examinations.

The most common forms of this pattern sequence the information in one of two ways: (1) problem-process-solution or (2) problem-cause-solution. Both patterns first describe the problem and then proceed through diagnosis and analysis to propose a solution. The diagnosis and analysis may include an evaluation of processes or procedures or a discussion of causes contributing to the problem.

For example, you might use this pattern to write a paper discussing how diabetes is being treated through diet, drugs, exercise, and surgery. Your process analysis would examine the progression of the disease and the different ways to treat it. In the problem-cause-solution pattern, you might describe why diabetes is a serious health problem and the known causes of diabetes, such as diet, genetics, biochemical processes, and obesity. Your proposed solution for preventing diabetes or mitigating its effects would then be based on what you know about these causes.

Discussing Raw Data

Some college writing requires that you interpret and discuss raw data presented in a non-textual form, such as a table, graph, figure, or illustration. You may have conducted a survey and now have to report on the results. Or you may be asked to support your position on capital punishment by citing data on recidivism in your state.

The organisation of a data discussion usually follows the general-to-specific pattern. First, you present the main claim supported by the data. Then, you discuss the details as they support or deny the main claim. Your discussion might include the problems, implications, exceptions, methodologies, and so on. Interpreting and commenting on data require clear thinking on your part, reflected in a clear thesis with specific supporting ideas for your interpretation of the data.

When asked to write this kind of an assignment, some students make the mistake of just describing what the data say, rather than interpreting the data. Another mistake is to read too much into the data and draw unreasonable conclusions. The key is "to find the right strength of claim for the data and then order your statements in some appropriate way or from the most emphatic to the least emphatic. Each discipline has its own methods, theories, beliefs, and common practices for working with data.

Summaries

Very likely, you will be asked sometime during your college career to write a *summary* of research sources, a procedure, a book, an article, or some other piece of information. Your summary may be presented orally, in writing, informally, formally, or for an exam. You may even be asked to summarise information in a graphical format.

Writing a summary is an opportunity for you to demonstrate your understanding of course material. Many students mistakenly think that simply repeating the key words from the material suffices. In summarising, not only are you asked to repeat in your own words what you know, but you may be asked to evaluate the summarised information or draw several ideas together in a summary.

Here are some tips for summarising:

— Always present a balanced view of your material.

— Always give equal coverage to all parts of the material.

— Always use a neutral tone in your writing.

— Always keep the author's material distortion-free.

— Always summarise in your own words.

Opening summaries give just the essential content, results, and conclusions and may be brief. Formal summaries, such as an executive summary, may be 1–5 percent of the original material in length and reflect the organisation of the original source. Remember that your purpose is to present faithfully the contents of the original source.

Abstracts, on the other hand, are used by readers to decide whether to read a source in full. They are compressed versions of the essential content of a source. Those who catalogue information and create research reference materials also use abstracts. Most information-retrieval systems can scan the key words in an abstract and retrieve the source it is based on. Most assuredly, you will write an abstract for a graduate thesis or dissertation.

Because abstracts help readers decide whether they want to read the original, the content is quite compressed. Your abstract will contain only a few sentences, perhaps only three to five. You should include the key words that reveal the major idea of the original material to identify the field of study involved.

Critiques

Many teachers regularly use *critiques* to find out whether you have read the material and to prepare you for exams. You could be asked to write critiques in any class. You may be asked to critique someone else's ideas, an excerpt, a book, a poem, a work of art, even a mathematical solution. Writing critiques improves your critical and analytical thinking and hones your evaluative skills.

When you write a critique, you must do justice to your material. The objective is to present the material fairly and then apply critical thinking and judgment to its ideas. Each discipline commonly uses its own methodology and language for critiques, so you should review critiques in your field and discuss them with your classmates or teacher to find good models. In fact, as part of your course work, you will probably learn the art of critiques in your specialisation.

In general, when you prepare to write a critique, you first read through the material. You'll want to decide the basis for your critique. What criteria and standards are you using to judge the material? Jot them down, spell them out clearly, and keep them in front of you while you draft your critique. Your critique may naturally take a general-to-specific organisation or even a problem-solution pattern.

Supporting with Research

When you express an opinion or make a statement, you improve your credibility with your reader by supporting what you say with research findings and examples. Using these findings along with other outside sources lends credence to your point of view. When you research topics, you will need to find out who the reliable sources are in the area of study. Some signs of reliability will be apparent to you when you first start your project.

Writing Essay Examinations

In addition to research papers, essay exams are among the more common college writing assignments. These exams not only call on most of your writing skills, they also test your ability to read carefully, understand the question, and write purposefully within a limited time. Weak essay exam answers are caused not so much by ignorance of the subject matter but by a lack of planning and strategy.

Many students complain that they perform their worst on essay exams, and the pressure of this forced and timed writing doesn't encourage a polished and well-thought out product. Often, students believe they must sacrifice planning time to a "data dump" to demonstrate what they know.

Too often students begin writing without first thinking about what they want to say and then developing their intentions into an adequate answer. The results are answers that are inadequate, unclear, often illogical, and irrelevant.

Read and Understand the Question

First, read the question carefully. If you misunderstand or misinterpret the question, your entire answer may miss the mark. Notice what the question requires you to do. Notice whether it asks you to *explain, discuss, summarise, define, evaluate, compare, analyse, or synthesise.* These key words help you to understand the question.

Essay questions are often broad questions that ask you to work with abstract terms, concepts, tendencies, or sweeping events or trends. They differ from short-answer questions in the level of specificate required in their answers. Short-answer questions usually ask that you recall information by providing facts, definitions, or examples.

Another way to understand essay questions is by understanding how they ask you to apply your knowledge, what rules and concepts you are being asked to use. If you are asked to *list, describe, explain, summarise, classify, apply, illustrate, use, calculate, sketch, or perform* an operation, you are being asked to apply particular knowledge you have acquired. If you are asked to *analyse, compare, contrast, evaluate, predict, determine cause and effect, synthesise, or evaluate,* you are being asked to select from the knowledge you have gained.

Essay questions usually call for some sort of application, analysis, synthesis, or evaluation of information, or some combination of these. Many students mistakenly summarise a plot or recapitulate the topic from the texts or class lectures in place of doing an analysis.

Organise Thinking Before Writing

Essay questions often fall into types calling for specific organisational strategies. For example, a question that asks you to compare and contrast two different architectural styles requires that you describe both styles and then discuss their similarities and differences.

On the other hand, a question that asks you to contrast these two architectural styles as expressions of the beliefs of the architects about what a house should be is asking you to look at the similarities and differences as aesthetic expressions of the philosophies of the two architects. In this case, you might discuss the characteristics of the different styles, one at a time, and then describe how these characteristics arise from the different views of what a house should be.

The types of questions presented here are typical of the kinds of essay questions on examinations or in course assignments. Notice that these assignments suggest certain strategies for developing your essay.

Essay Question Types Cause effect: What are the causes of the current crisis in the Asian market, and what effects will the crisis have on the European Economic Community? Discussion: Identify three of Kant's categorical imperatives and discuss them in relation to twentieth-century life. Demonstration: Demonstrate the feasibility of enterprise zones in cities with under 300,000 population and crumbling infrastructure. Evaluation: Evaluate Leakey's contribution to anthropology in light of at least two major criticisms levelled against him. Explication: Explain (explicate) the importance of the line "Turning and turning in the widening goer" in Years's poem "Second Coming." Process analysis: Describe the process associated with regenerating tissue after surgery to correct mitro valve prolapse.

Compare/contrast: Contrast the architectural styles of Frank Lloyd Right and Le Carburize as expressions of their beliefs of what a house should be. Synthesis: How does the individualism of Theory and Emersion differ? How do their notions of individualism differ from today's individualism?

Think through your general answer before you begin to develop your essay. Identify the strategy that is suggested or directed. If you cannot figure out exactly what your teacher is asking of you, ask for an explanation. When you decide on a specific rephrasing of the question, then write that down in the form of a thesis statement or topic sentence. Express your thesis as a probing question, if necessary, to begin exploring and discovering your ideas.

Make lists of related ideas that suggest themselves to you from your thesis statement. Ask yourself the journalist's questions to get your ideas flowing. Use the multiple perspectives strategy to look at the subject from different points of view. For most students, making lists, brainstorming, or using one of the formal idea-generating techniques will be enough to suggest a direction.

Make Answer Relevant and Complete

Writing a complete and relevant answer means that you addressed the question and organised your thoughts so that you included the information you needed to write during the time given to you. An essay exam, on the other hand, requires a discussion of the question to show your ability to select and organise information to support your thesis.

A Word About Style, Voice, and Tone

Style, voice, and tone in writing express the attitude of a writer at that moment and in relation to a particular subject and audience. Students often confuse writing style with some vague sense of personal style, or personality. But style is a technical term for the effect a writer can create through attitude, language, and the mechanics of writing. If the writing reflects a consistent choice of patterns, then it is perceived as coherent and harmonious, the style supporting the content. The writer's purpose and style clearly have a cause-and-effect relationship.

Voice and tone reflect your attitude about your subject and your readers. Voice is who the readers hear talking in your paper, and tone is the way in which you are doing the writing. Voice can be institutional or academic—that is, objective and formal. Or voice can be personal—in fact, your distinct voice. Do you want to inform your readers or to persuade them in some way? Your style and attitude toward your subject combine to create your voice and tone.

Your goal in college writing is to understand the material of your discipline and be able to discuss it effectively in writing. Your teachers want facts as well as opinions, and they want to be able to assess, through your writing, how well you synthesise your thinking and learning in the course. Your goal in most academic writing is to convey facts about a subject, integrate opinions based on facts, and synthesise what you have learned as you go along. You will discover, however, that some academic writing is persuasive and that your teachers will expect you to know the language of persuasion as well.

Style Through Vocabulary and Diction

Many disciplines have their own vocabulary of special terms that you learn as you study each discipline. The way you use a special vocabulary affects the style and tone of your writing. The longer you study the discipline and the more you read, the better you will become at mastering its vocabulary.

Students may get into trouble because they do not know the vocabulary of a discipline. They may use ordinary words where special words are needed, or their writing may simply become vague. Teachers may identify such writing by inserting in the margin comments, such as *vague diction, poor word choice,* or even *inappropriate style.*

The following hypothetical examples from two papers on reducing defects in software development show you what a difference vocabulary can make in establishing style, tone, and credibility for each writer. To make up for her lack of appropriate words, and thus of clear thought, she uses vague terms to establish criteria, such as *bad* and *worse*, and falls back on cliches, such as *rocket science*. The second writer, on the other hand, has mastered the few special words he needs to express the concepts taught in class and to draw conclusions from what he has learned.

Vocabulary is related to diction, another important element of style. Where *vocabulary* refers to the specific words in a discipline, diction refers to the overall selection of language for your writing. Words are not right and wrong in and of themselves. If your purpose is to present your thesis and research so that your reader will find your position credible, then your diction should be appropriate—objective, concrete, and specific.

Finally, style rests on language. Poor style and unacceptable tone do impede communication and may affect your grade. You should cultivate a style that shows your knowledge and command of course material and that enables you to convey opinions about what you have learned in a manner that audiences, including your teacher, will appreciate.

Here are some practical suggestions for developing a style that supports your content and your thinking:

— Let your purpose guide your writing. Your style is the result of your control over your content, not added later to give your writing "personality." Know what you want to accomplish with your content, and your style will take care of itself.

— In general, choose a style between colloquial and formal. This moderate style will work in most cases where your assignment does not specifically call for a colloquial or formal style.

— Keep your style consistent in tone and diction by carefully choosing the patterns of writing and vocabulary that best serve your purpose.

— Try to anticipate how your reader will understand your writing. Be specific and concrete and avoid wordiness.

Academic Integrity and Documentation

In writing from source materials, integrity is the standard. Integrity and documentation are interrelated. Without standards for academic honesty, documenting sources has little meaning.

Plagiarism is the presentation of another person's idea or product as one's own. Plagiarism includes copying verbatim all or parts of another person's work; using phrases, charts, figures, illustrations, computer programs, or mathematical or scientific solutions without citing the source; paraphrasing ideas, conclusions, or research without citing the source.

Students can avoid unintentional plagiarism by carefully following accepted scholarly practices. Notes taken for papers and research projects should accurately record sources of material to be cited, quoted, paraphrased, or summarised, and papers should acknowledge those sources in footnotes.

In general, you should:

— Acknowledge the source of all evidence, from rumours to formal documents. Also acknowledge all outside help, whether from a person; an electronic source, such as a Web site, an e-mail communication, or a list serve; and any other source.

— Consider everything in print or electronic format as protected by copyright.

— Document all written, filmed, video-taped, audio-taped, and electronic sources of information.

— Use the documentation style appropriate for your discipline.

Giving Credit

Plagiarism means presenting other people's ideas as your own. It is a serious offence against academic and personal integrity that may result in a failing grade or expulsion.

Not all students understand plagiarism, and some are surprised when they are accused of committing it. The mistake made most often is failure to realise that *any* borrowed material should be documented, even if it is very familiar to you. Your course textbook, for example, should be cited properly when you quote or summarise from it in a research paper. And, even if you change the words of the text to your own, you still are required to provide proper citations.

Plagiarism represents a disconnected kind of thinking characterised by patching the works of others together without a coherent thesis. If you start with your own research question, you then easily find ways to use your sources to support your point of view. Once you begin with your research inquiry, then, plagiarism becomes a technical problem, one that is solvable by simply learning the rules for documenting research sources and when to apply them.

Documentation

Without doubt, the best way to avoid plagiarism and adhere to copyright law is to give credit to others whose work you use or refer to. Doing so involves keeping careful records of your sources and documenting these sources using a style guide. When you document your sources, you create a path that your readers and other researchers can follow to understand how you derived your findings.

Documentation acknowledges indebtedness to one's sources. It's expected that students, as well as writers, researchers, scholars, and scientists, declare such indebtedness.

Keeping Accurate Records

Keeping good records is essential to help you guard against plagiarism. Your records may take the form of note cards, bibliographic cards, your research log, or even photocopies of articles or pages. Always note whether you are quoting, paraphrasing, or summarising information you found or musing about the information.

Using carefully organised note cards can also help you guard against plagiarism and even help you develop your own ideas while you are researching. Some guidelines for using note cards are listed below:

- Use 4-by-6 cards for taking notes—these accommodate longer notes.
- Write with ink—pencil often smudges and becomes unreadable.
- Write only a single idea on each note card. If your notes require more than one card, staple them together. Staple personal comment note cards to the source card to which they refer.
- Write the source of the note in the upper left corner and the topic, context, or general heading in the upper right corner.
- Use note cards for summaries, paraphrases, quotations, and personal comments.

The following sample note card contains the pertinent information one writer will need later when he or she has integrated these notes into the final research paper. It's important that the writer introduce the quotation in the context of the idea being developed and then place quotation marks around the exact quotation, noting the author and page number so he or she can easily document the sources later.

You will also want to make note cards with your personal comments to help you recall what you were thinking when you were researching. Personal comments can be your questions, ideas, conclusions, explanations of terms or ideas, clarification of an issue, or even new ideas. Here is a sample note card with a personal comment. Notice that the note card is marked as "personal comment."

Remember the main reasons you are keeping accurate records: first, you are acknowledging your sources, and, second, you are giving your readers a trail to those sources so they can understand and evaluate your thinking.

In summary, here is what is usually required to provide a path to your sources:

— author's last name and first name or initials
— title of the source and edition
— date of publication, along with edition, if appropriate
— publisher and location
— page number(s) of material cited

Managing Source Material

There are three ways to use sources in research writing: quoting, paraphrasing, and summarising. To help you avoid misusing them, we will discuss how to use sources and when. In each and every case, you need to cite your source.

Quoting Sources

When you want the exact phrasing and pattern of thinking or wording of your source, quote it verbatim. You use quotations in your writing when you need to invoke the authority of your source, to preserve the qualities of the written language, or when the original material is so well phrased that a summary or paraphrase just won't capture the ideas.

The following example shows you how to include a quote from your source material. The sentences preceding the quotation are in the writer's own words and are used to provide a context for the quotation, which is then used to support the writer's thoughts and expound on them with authority.

In-Text or Parenthetical Citations

MLA Style

The MLA style has been using the parenthetical documentation since 1983. In this style, Arabic numerals are used, the letter *p.* Or *pp.* For page numbers is omitted, *line* or *lines* is used to note lines of text, and the bibliography is headed "Works Cited."

The MLA style permits a shorthand method for identifying in your paper the author and the page number of the work if you are using only one book by that author. Because in the field of humanities there is less concern for the currency of references, the date is usually omitted in the in-text citation.

When the readers of your paper go to your bibliography, they discover the full reference to Paul Lauter's essay. The entries here are in alphabetical order using the author's last name, are double-spaced, and have a flush and hanging or hanging indent in the second and subsequent lines.

In-Text or Parenthetical Citations

APA Style

The APA style, established by the American Psychological Association, is the most widely used documentation style. You'll want to use this style unless your teacher specifies otherwise. APA requires that you use Arabic numbers, *p.* Or *pp.* For page numbers, and a list of references for the citations.

When students write a paper or a thesis, they are producing what the APA style manual calls a "final" manuscript. Students who are required to use APA style should get clarification from their teachers about whether they are expected to use the style for students' papers or the style for "copy" manuscript, which is prepared for journal publication and must undergo type setting. Many teachers don't realise that APA makes such distinctions. For example, in journal submissions, APA style requires that reference list entries for articles be double-spaced. For reference lists in student manuscripts, APA style permits the entry to be single-spaced. Another difference is that reference lists for student manuscripts contain only the references cited in the text, unless there is a specific requirement to give evidence that students have read more widely or are more widely knowledgeable about the field.

Although most of the APA style manual discusses the correct style for copy manuscripts, the in-text citations are the same for both students' assignments and journal article manuscripts read by editors and reviewers. These journal article manuscripts are then typeset to conform to the specific style of the publications for which they are prepared.

Unlike MLA style, however, the APA style is concerned about dates and requires that the author and date of a source be mentioned in the citation. Notice that the APA style uses commas to separate the elements of the citation.

Chicago Style

The *Chicago Manual*, long used by those in the physical and natural sciences, shares some similarities with APA and MLA styles in its use of note citations. Chicago favours the author-date citation within the text in parentheses, but also includes page numbers as an option. Like MLA style, Full bibliographic citations are then amplified in the list of references. Chicago favours the APA format of hanging indents—indenting the second and subsequent lines of the entries. Bibliographies are not a requirement.

In-Text or Parenthetical Citations

CBE Style

The CBE style manual, written by the Council of Biology Editors in 1994, is used to advise writers in the natural sciences—such as biology, biotechnology, and medicine—about style and formatting of scientific papers, journals, and books for publications.

The CBE manual, *Scientific Style and Format: The CBE Manual for Authors, Editors, and Publishers,* recommends two methods for citing and documenting sources.

— the name-year system and

— the citation-sequence system.

The name-year system is based on the APA; the citation-sequence system lists the sources in numerical sequence based on their occurrences in the scientific paper and keys all in-text citations to that list.

Since there are two systems, you'll need to ask your teacher which he or she prefers. Keep in mind that the target journal for publication may still dictate any modification to these systems to meet editorial guidelines.

Citing World Wide Web Sources

Some students believe that Web sources have no copyright and that information found on the Web may be used without acknowledging the source.

When you include information from the Web in your paper, therefore, provide a complete citation. You want to be able to direct your reader to find the source you cited. According to the UMUC Office of Library Services your Web citation should contain the following information:

— *Author*—Creator or compiler of the information; may include the Web master or the organisation.

— *Year, month, date*— the Web page was put online; should be the same as the "last updated" date if available.

— *Title*—the document, usually found at the top of the Web page.

— *Type of medium*—Way the document was accessed. If found on the Web or through another Internet service, this should be "Online."

— *Site/path/file*—Address or URL of the Web site.

— *Access date*— you viewed the Web page or accessed the information.

CBE Style Manual

The CBE style manual, written by the Council of Biology Editors in 1994, is used to advise writers in the natural sciences—such as biology, biotechnology, and medicine—about style and formatting of scientific papers, journals, and books for publications.

The CBE manual, *Scientific Style and Format: The CBE Manual for Authors, Editors, and Publishers,* recommends two methods for citing and documenting sources,

> the name-year system and
> the citation-sequence system.

The name-year system is based on the APA; the citation-sequence system lists the sources in numerical sequence based on their occurrences in the scientific paper and keys all in-text citations to that list.

Since there are two systems, you'll need to ask your teacher which he or she prefers. Keep in mind that the target journal for publication may still dictate any modification to these systems to meet editorial guidelines.

Bibliographies and Source Lists

A bibliography is a list of books and other references an author has used in a research paper. This list may be titled Bibliography, Selected Bibliography, or Works Consulted, depending on the style manual you are using. For these lists, the author includes references not specifically cited in the text but consulted for general information.

Bibliographies are usually placed at the ends of papers. If your research paper has chapters, you would include a list of references at the end of the chapter for the works cited in that chapter.

A special kind of bibliography, the *annotated bibliography*, is often used to direct your readers to other books and resources on your topic. Such bibliographies offer a few lines of information about each source. Your teacher may ask you to write an informal literature review or a bibliographical essay using an annotated bibliography. By surveying the literature broadly, you can begin to narrow down a topic for your research assignment.

Your bibliography may be on note cards that can be rearranged as your priorities change or on the computer so you can print out the entire list when you are doing research. As you compile your notes for your research and narrow down your ideas, your bibliography will evolve until you have the final bibliography for your research.

Integrating Sources

In general, you should strive to make your presence known in your writing and not let your sources of information dominate the content. To do this, you must be the stage manager. Thus, with your management, your reader becomes aware of the voices of other authorities. The following suggestions may help you avoid overseeing your sources when you write:

— Always introduce a paragraph with a sentence that you believe is your own thought on the subject matter. This sentence can be a topic sentence that makes a transition from the ideas of the preceding paragraph to new ideas or evidence or one that states a hypothesis that you want to prove within the paragraph.

— Avoid long quotations that are not surrounded by your own interpretation or opinion. You should examine the number and nature of quotations after writing the paper to detect overuse or inappropriate use.

— Avoid using sources you don't understand because you will have to use someone else's words to integrate the source into your paper.

— Do not allow your readers to interpret too much on their own. Avoid the temptation to include uncommented-on quotations simply for effect.

> Never include quotations that do not add to your paper's argument, even though they may prove that you have done research. Even when your teacher requires you to refer to a specified number of outside resources, always include only those references that add value to your paper.

A good practice is to acknowledge all sources from which you borrow. However, you don't need to cite sources for familiar proverbs or aphorisms, such as A stitch in time saves nine, Art imitates life, or Feed a cold; starve a fever. Nor do you need to cite sources for common knowledge, such as Abraham Lincoln was assassinated by John W'lkes Booth while attending a performance at Ford's Theatre or The sum of the angles of any right triangle equals 180 degrees. This is a case when it is better to err on the side of caution than to leave out the appropriate documentation and possibly commit plagiarism.

Another kind of plagiarism is turning in a paper that you have purchased or borrowed from someone else or that you have written for a previous class or a current class. Such behaviour is simply academic dishonesty in a broad form. All colleges and universities have documented requirements for academic integrity that are stringently enforced. In general, the penalty for deliberate plagiarism is expulsion. In almost every instance if you plagiarise you will fail the course in which you plagiarised, and there may be other penalties.

Assessing Your Writing

Assessing your writing requires discipline, patience, and self-examination at every stage. In addition, you must understand the process of writing a paper to realise what it is you must evaluate. To assess your writing, you must evaluate both your writing process and your written product using a selected list of criteria. Assessment is not simply answering yes to a series of questions on a checklist. Each time you write an essay assignment or a research paper, you become more skilled at understanding the writing process and how it works for you.

The Research Stage

In this stage, you should emphasise the nature and scope of your research, ensuring that you have kept orderly and complete notes, performed an adequate survey of the research, and have your supporting ideas ready to develop into your first draft. In the research stage, you should be able to answer in detail the following questions:

Checklist for the Research Stage

1. How [well] does my research question describe the scope and slant of my topic?

2. How extensive is my initial survey of possible resources for my topic?
3. Are my research notes methodical, complete, and orderly? Are they clear about what is quoted, paraphrased, and summarised from my research?
4. What other idea-generating techniques did I use—brainstorming, keeping a journal or research log, free writing?
5. Are my bibliography notes complete with all citations and bibliographical data on every source, and are they representative of the survey of my topic?

The Draft Stage

When writing the first draft, you are trying to discover your thinking and to explore the ideas you have developed. In this stage, you should use your working thesis to plan your organisation and develop your thoughts. In the draft stage, you should be able to answer the following questions with authority:

— Can I state the thesis specifically and summarise the one main idea to discuss?

— Does my thesis statement suggest my writing strategy and what patterns I might use to develop my ideas?

— Can I support my thesis with evidence from class readings, research notes, experience, or all of these?

The First Draft

When the first draft is ready for review and feedback, you can use a checklist like the one presented here or develop one of your own. By identifying the stage in which errors most often occur, you can return to that stage for revision.

Planning and Researching Phases

— Is the thesis statement clear and focused on one major idea?

— Are the intent and purpose clearly expressed?

— Is the target audience clearly defined?

— Does the scope seem appropriate for this writing project?

— Is sufficient information provided?
— Does the paper consider other perspectives or address possible questions?
— Are facts and opinions explained and supported in convincing detail?

Organising and Drafting Phases

— Is the controlling idea sufficiently developed?
— Are the major parts clearly defined and logically sequence to fit the purpose?
— Do the minor ideas clearly support the major statements?
— Does the introduction clearly set the stage by announcing the controlling idea?
— Does the conclusion return to the controlling idea and review the major parts?

Using Feedback

When you solicit feedback, you need to evaluate it for its relevance to your assignment. Of course, you need to pay attention to your teacher's feedback, but all feedback is not relevant to your revision.

The Revision Process

After you have revised your first draft, the major issues of content, organisation, and style should be clearly worked out. This stage of assessment is necessarily at a higher level or is more general because you should expect to have addressed the more detailed aspects during the other stages of writing.

Checklist for Revising the Final Paper

Understanding the Assignment

— Did I demonstrate that I understood the requirements of the assignment?
— Did I demonstrate an understanding of the skills and techniques needed to complete this assignment?

— Did I demonstrate that I understood the readings relevant to this assignment?

— Did I demonstrate an understanding of the concepts and methods in my discipline?

Content/Substance

— Is the assignment complete?

— Is the information appropriate for the assignment?

— Did I use quotations, paraphrases, and summaries appropriately?

— Are my citations and references in the correct style for my discipline?

Organisation

— Is the order of the information logical?

— Are the introduction and conclusion clear and related?

— Does the organisation pattern reflect my critical thinking strategy?

Style

— Do the transitions clearly act as verbal signals?

— Do I use logical connections and summarise when necessary?

— Is my style readable and coherent?

— Is the tone expressive and consistent?

Diction

— Are my tone and diction appropriate to my audience?

— Is my English clear and emphatic?

— Is my vocabulary appropriately formal or informal for this assignment?

Format

— Is the format appropriate and conventional for this assignment?

— Does the format of the assignment promote quick, clear understanding?

— Do the graphics clarify the text?

Correctness/Mechanics

— Is my paper free of spelling, grammatical, and punctuation errors?

— Do I use standard English?

— Do I use appropriate typography for the final printing?

Grading of Writing

Students often want to know how their writing assignments are graded—that is, what is an *A* paper, a *B* paper, and so on. If you are in doubt, ask your teacher to explain his or her grading system. If your teacher gives you no feedback other than a grade, you should inquire about the strengths and weaknesses of your assignment.

The following grading criteria are considered standard for writing assignments. You can apply these criteria to your writing and use them along with any specific requirements your teacher issues for each assignment, to help you determine your grade for any individual assignment. Remember that your teacher may give you a separate list of criteria or an additional list of requirements.

Grade of A

An *A* paper is characterised by outstanding informative writing marked by superior readability and competent handling of content. These traits are demonstrated in the following ways:

— The substance and organisation follow a clear, logical sequence that makes the information easily accessible to the reader.

— The purpose is clearly expressed, and the selected details of the assignment reflect this purpose.

— The audience is accommodated throughout the assignment as reflected in effective communication and style.

— Words are chosen and sentences are constructed to make the information understandable.

— The grammar, mechanics, and format are flawless.

***Grade of* B**

A *B* paper is characterised by distinguished writing that successfully fulfils the requirements but contains one of the following weaknesses:

— Although the writing is essentially well organised, the audience analysis, the statement of purpose, or the handling of the content is flawed.

— Although sentences are grammatically correct, their structure or length or both sometimes cause readers to work unnecessarily hard.

— Ambiguous or vague wording hinders precise communication.

— A small lapse in audience accommodation causes reader distraction.

— Grammar, mechanics, and format flaws interfere with reading and comprehension.

***Grade of* C**

A *C* paper is characterised by satisfactory writing that is generally effective but contains any one of the following weaknesses:

— Although satisfactorily written, the body of the assignment is not clearly organised, or some material is not clearly explained; the audience and purpose are not clear.

— Sentences, although they are grammatically correct, often make information difficult to extract; editing key words or converting nouns to verbs could solve such problems.

— Wording interferes with readability, but the reader can still glean the meaning; rereading is often required.

— Repeated grammar, mechanics, or format errors mar the paper.

Grade of D

A *D* paper struggles to communicate information and contains weak writing. In a professional working environment, such writing would be considered incompetent because it suffers from any one of the following problems:

- Any two of the problems listed under a *C* paper.
- Minimal evidence of audience accommodation.
- Serious wording problems, such as garbled wording, gives the reader repeated and serious difficulties in understanding.
- Serious sentence problems, such as run-on sentences and comma splices, damage the readability.
- Grammar, spelling, or format problems create frequent obstacles to understanding.

Grade of F

A failing grade on a writing assignment usually means that your paper contains any two problems from the list for a *D* paper.

A General Assessment Tool

Some teachers who are not writing teachers use a single-page evaluation tool to give their students feedback on their writing. We are including here an evaluation tool that you or your teacher can use for your writing assignments. One way to use this tool is to assign each criterion a value.

General Assessment of a Writing Assignment

Understanding the Assignment

- Student demonstrates an understanding of the assignment.
- Student demonstrates an understanding of the skills and techniques needed to complete the assignment.
- Student demonstrates an understanding of the reading assignments relevant to this assignment.

Substance

- Student clearly indicates a knowledge of the subject matter and has made the information accessible to the reader.
- Student has focused the subject on a single, appropriate thesis.
- Audience is targeted properly.
- Purpose of the content is clear.

Organisation

— Student's intentions and methods in developing the content are clear.

— Controlling idea is sufficiently developed.

Organisation is logical and follows a clear sequence.

— Major and minor supports are clearly defined for the reader.

— Introductions, transitions, and conclusions are clear, logical, and contain relevant information.

Style

— Diction is appropriate to the audience and its level of technical expertise.

— Level of details presented is appropriate and consistent.

— Overall tone is consistent and appropriate to the audience and subject matter.

— Sentences are structured effectively and correctly.

— Document design and presentation are appropriate to the audience and subject matter.

Correctness

— Student has used correct grammar and effective sentence structures.

— Punctuation is correct.

— Document fits the expected format, and the appearance is professional

Summary Comments

It's important to summarise your overall impression of the paper, as well as its strengths and weaknesses.

Writing use of Assessment to Improve Your Writing

When you have successfully completed a writing assignment, you have begun to improve as a writer. When you choose to evaluate your writing, you have contracted with yourself to improve it. Even if you do not choose a career in professional writing, you will derive greater satisfaction from your academic and workplace writing if you continue to improve your writing skills.

By identifying your strengths and weaknesses and working on improving specific aspects of your writing using a list of criteria and a plan, you are using assessment to improve your writing.

Here's how to continue improving your writing:

(i) Learn from your mistakes. Watch for patterns of strengths and weaknesses in your writing. Consciously and methodically work on improving your weaknesses. Regularly use your strengths to keep them strong.

(ii) Analyse examples of good writing. By understanding how other writers have succeeded in writing effectively, you can improve your skills and strategies. Keep a notebook of writing samples that includes your notations about what works and what doesn't.

(iii) Build your skills as you go along. Work methodically on your writing, focusing on specific skills each time you write a paper. Keep a journal or course notebook so you can practice writing in a specific discipline. Don't wait until the last minute to work on your writing assignments.

(iv) Find opportunities for writing practice. Some courses require you to keep a journal or notebook with review and integrating questions, case study discussions, or laboratory notes. Use these opportunities to practice writing topic sentences, thesis statements, and major and minor supports. Practice writing effective sentences in a unified paragraph or practice free writing. Use these shorter assignments as warm-ups for the longer research papers.

(v) Look for writing opportunities in all your classes. When you participate in a group assignment, volunteer to take minutes or write summaries of group decisions. Produce written proceedings of oral presentations.

(vi) Take writing courses beyond your requirements. All writing courses, including creative writing, will help you improve your writing skills. Take a variety of writing courses to help you broaden your vocabulary, style, sentence structure, organisation, and thinking.

(vii) Take writing seminars offered by professional organisations. Many professional organisations offer short writing courses to help you learn new skills or new kinds of writing.

(viii)Keep a journal or writing log. Keep tabs of your writing plan and your improvement. Set aside 10 or 15 minutes daily to review what you are focusing on and practising; set aside another 10 or 15 minutes to practice it.

(ix) Write, You won't learn to write by reading a book on writing if you don't practice what you have learned. Learning to write is like learning to play an instrument: you get better only by setting your goals and practising your lessons.

(x) Read, read. By reading good writing, you will be able to identify solid writing models and improve your sentence structure, spelling, punctuation, and vocabulary.

Collaborative Writing and Peer Reviewing

Many college writing assignments require that you work in a project. Collaborative writing and peer reviewing are not the same tasks, although both are often treated as collaborative writing. Collaborative, or team, writirg is the process of producing a written work as a group where all team members contribute to the content and the decisions about how the group will function. Because many teachers give peer review assignments as well as collaborative ones, we offer some tips for those as well.

Group assignments can be difficult for many adult students with busy schedules because they require planning, coordination, and frequent communication with other students. Teachers nonetheless view group work as good preparation for the types of complex assignments you are likely to receive on the job. Also, collaborative assignments offer students the benefits and experience of building on existing knowledge through the dynamic interplay with and among other students, the subject matter, and the teacher. This appendix presents some strategies that can help you make collaborative writing and peer reviewing assignments successful.

Peer Reviewing

When a classmate asks you to review his or her paper and provide feedback, you should take that task seriously. Many students want honest feedback on their writing and feel cheated if they receive cursory, highly critical, or highly uncritical feedback on their work. Obtaining a peer review is an opportunity to test your writing before you turn it in for a grade. Feedback may be verbal or written. Here are some guidelines you and your classmates can use to review one another's writing:

1. Exchange copies of your writing with your peers.
2. Review and comment on the paper by writing brief, specific comments in the margins. Place a check mark by a good point and an *x* by an error or problem point.
3. Pay attention to larger issues: don't worry about smaller details, such as punctuation and spelling at this point. Circle them and move on.
4. Number the paragraphs as you read them so you can refer to the numbers when critiques the organisation and the logic of development in your summary comments.
5. Write summary comments at the end, addressing the larger issues, such as clarity, conciseness, accuracy, and readability. Sign and date your copy and return it to the writer.

For those whose papers are being reviewed, the job of listening to feedback is an active and engaging, but quiet job. When you hand over your paper to a peer reviewer, don't spend time apologising for its content or your presentation of the information. Above all, your responsibility is to listen carefully to the feedback and take notes for future revisions. Don't interrupt the reviewer except to ask for clarification.

Writing Plan

The collaborative group assignment is intended to be one where the entire team contributes to the writing. The key ingredients of successful group work are leadership, planning, effective communication, equal division of labour, and equal sharing of responsibilities for results, as well as courtesy, thoughtfulness, and dependability.

For group writing projects, planning is especially important because writers tend to write in solitude from established plans and directions. When due dates are met, the work stays on schedule. A writing plan should include the following:

— description of the final project
— criteria for success
— content outline
— assignment of responsibilities for sections of content
— schedule for finishing parts
— editing and reviewing strategy
— production information

Issues to Resolve

In addition, writing groups should discuss and resolve ahead of time some of the following issues:

— when and where to meet as a group or how to meet when the participants are in a distance education class
— how to send materials between participants in the most efficient way
— what to do if someone has to drop out or falls behind
— what the group expects to get as a grade and the ways in which each member will evaluate the others
— who communicates with the teacher, and how that will occur
— how differences of opinion will be resolved
— what roles the group members will assume

Groups should also plan to exchange contact information and should discuss technical considerations, such as how the writing will be merged into a single project, what word processing and graphics software will be used, what style guide will be followed, and who will make decisions about editorial and content disputes.

Assignments

Often, a team can manage the collaborative assignment by using some group reporting techniques from the workplace. By planning the writing and reporting regularly to your teacher, you can keep the project on target and get guidance from your teacher when you need it. As a team, your collaborative writing group should plan to write the following for your assignment:

— progress report memo with subsequent informal progress reports submitted weekly
— editing strategy for your group project
— information plan to manage the project
— formal progress report
— review draft
— final project
— evaluation for each team member

Methodology

When the major writing project is a collaborative one, first form a writing team and work together to produce a collaborative project. Each member should plan to be responsible for at least two roles on the writing team, (1) writing a specific section of the project and (2) serving as a specialist in one or more areas concerning the project. This coordination requires courtesy, thoughtful communication, and dependability on everyone's part.

Each student should keep his or her own copy of the entire assignment, with its parts, together in a portfolio or notebook as the group completes the individual assignments. The group then turns in the completed project in hard copy. If a Web format is required, then prepare an HTML version for the Web.

Each team member should plan to write a specific section of the project— some members may write more than others depending on their roles. Roles may overlap or be shared, depending on team members' skills. Each student should take on two or more of the following roles:

— *Writer:* Everyone in the group writes and revises a specific part of the project.
— *Group Leader:* This person coordinates the team, organises the writing plan and schedule and picks up loose ends.

— *Editor*: This person edits and proofreads final drafts, provides stylistic standards for the group as a whole, and guides the group in using stylistic conventions and formats.
— *Graphics Layout Artist and Production Manager:* This person is responsible for project design, illustrations, layout, hard-copy and Web formats, and the printing of the final project.
— *Subject Matter Specialist:* Each person is responsible for research on technical topics, assisting team members with technical problems, and testing the final project for accuracy. All members must become subject matter specialists in at least one area.
— *Web master:* In Web projects, this person is responsible for putting the project on the Web and administering it.

Your teacher may act as manager or ask that you manage your own team writing assignment. In either case, you should plan to meet as a group and decide which roles each of you will fulfil on the team and which sections of the project each of you will write. Be sure your teacher gets copies of all of them. The tasks described here should help you manage your team writing. Plan to write all or some of them as a group.

Tasks of Members of Collaborative Writing Groups

1. *Informal progress report in the form of a memo:* At the first group meeting, members present their backgrounds and what they are most interested in doing for this project. At the end of the meeting, the team writes a group progress report identifying each person's background and desired roles, describing briefly your group's technical writing/editing and production environment, and any questions, problems, or bright ideas that emerge.
2. *Subsequent informal progress reports:* Thereafter, members submit weekly informal progress reports about attendance, action items, progress, and assignments. One person should act as recorder for the group during your discussion and take notes for the progress report.
3. *Editing strategy:* To plan for reviewing and revising the final draft, your team must think of ways to evaluate and edit your team writing. This strategy should address the needs of hard-copy as

well as Web formats if you are doing a Web project. Your editing strategy should identify the project's readers, purpose, and uses identify the ways in which both substantive and copy editing problems will be resolved present a schedule for reviews and editing describe how the final changes will be implemented

In essence, your team has to anticipate many of the pitfalls of writing your project. Because most editing strategies focus on copy editing or substantive editing your editing strategy can be written before your project is complete.

1. *Information plan:* An initial planning tool, this information plan includes a purpose definition, scope definition, audience analysis, objectives, statement of purpose, production and distribution plan, tentative schedule for completing each project piece, and list of specific tasks assigned to each group member. Discuss and write this plan as a group.
2. *Formal progress report or updated revision of the information plan:* This report describes the project status and significant deviations from the initial plan and presents a revised project schedule. Submit the revised plan with a one-page memo that describes what the changes are about midway through your project.
3. *Review draft:* This draft includes each section of your assignment with an example of the final project design and any graphics. If you have not yet completed a section, make space for it in your project and describe what will be in that section, how you will implement the content, and when you think it will be finished. Based on this draft, your teacher can now approve your draft or make recommendations or both.
4. *Final project:* No doubt, there will be content requirements for your final project. For example, a formal report might include a title page, a transmittal letter, a table of contents, the body of the report, and any appendices.
5. *Evaluation for each team member:* Every member of the team should plan on evaluating the other members in a brief paragraph. You will need to be specific and honest here so that your teacher can grade the project fairly.

Sample Informal Progress Report

The informal progress report should be in the form of a weekly memo that tells your teacher what progress your group has made on the assignment. Use a standard memo format, but consider designing your own group logo or style for the memo. These reports should contain the following information:

— list of attends at any group meeting that was held, list of who missed it and why, and statement of whether or not the absence was excused

— list of agenda action items

— list of decisions made about your action items

status report to date for each participant

— list of tentative action items for the next meeting

Members of the team should initial or sign off on each progress report. Include members' names and contact numbers, including phone numbers and e-mail addresses, so that your teacher can easily contact you or your group as needed

Peer Evaluation

Your group should discuss the criteria on which you will evaluate one another. Items you might want to include are listed below.

— Fulfilment of agreed-upon responsibilities

— dependability

— cooperation

— effort

— quality and level of work

— ability to meet deadlines

— attendance at meetings

— timeliness of contributions

You should decide what it means to meet these criteria successfully and what constitutes failure. Your team might consider a separate evaluation form for your leader. The criteria to consider for a project leader's evaluation might be:

— ability to lead
— fairness in assigning tasks
— ability to resolve conflicts
— ability to motivate
— attendance at meetings

The ability to collaborate in a team project is an invaluable skill in today's workplace. Although many students will benefit by this experience, many will struggle to participate successfully. It's in everyone's interest to have a strong project team.

Basic Paragraph Structure

The Topic Sentence

A topic sentence usually comes at the beginning of a paragraph; that is, it is usually the first sentence in a formal academic paragraph. Not only is a topic sentence the first sentence of a paragraph, but, more importantly, it is the most general sentence in a paragraph. What does "most general" mean? It means that there are not many details in the sentence, but that the sentence introduces an overall idea that you want to discuss later in the paragraph.

For example, suppose that you want to write a paragraph about the natural landmarks of your hometown. The first part of your paragraph might look like this:

> My hometown is famous for several amazing natural features. First, it is noted for the Wheaten River, which is very wide and beautiful. Also, on the other side of the town is Wheaten Hill, which is unusual because it is very steep.

Note how the first sentence, *My hometown, Wheaten, is famous for several amazing geographical features, is* the most general statement. This sentence is different from the two sentences that follow it, since the second and third sentences mention specific details about the town's geography, and are not general statements.

Here are some examples of sentences that cannot be used as topic sentences. Can you figure out why they are inappropriate?

1 My hometown is famous because it is located by Wheaten River, which is very wide, and because it is built near an unusually steep hill called Wheaten Hill.

2. There are two reasons why some people like to buy cars with automatic transmission and two reasons why others like cars with manual transmission.

3. Clouds are white.

The problem with sentence #1 is that it contains too many details. Topic sentences are general, and details should appear later in the paragraph. A better topic sentence would be like the one mentioned above, *My hometown is famous for several amazing geographical features.*

Sentence #2 is not appropriate as a topic sentence because it mentions two topics, not just one.

The problem with sentence #3 is that it is *too general*. It is also very boring! Would you like to read a paragraph with this topic sentence? Most people would not.

We can rewrite sentences #2 and #3 in the following ways to make it better:

> There are two reasons why some people like to buy cars with automatic transmission. *OR (in a different paragraph): There* are two reasons why some people like cars with manual transmission.
> The shapes of clouds are determined by various factors.

Supporting Sentences

Consider again the above-mentioned, short paragraph:

> My hometown, Wheaten, is famous for several amazing natural features. First, it is noted for the Wheaten River, which is very wide and beautiful. Also, on the other side of the town is Wheaten Hill, which is unusual because it is very steep.

When a reader reads a topic sentence, such as *My hometown, Wheaten, is famous for several amazing natural features, a* question should usually appear in the reader's mind. In this case, the question should be like, "What are the natural features that make Wheaten famous?" The reader should then expect that the rest of the paragraph will give an answer to this question.

Now look at the sentences after the topic sentence. We can see that the second sentence in the paragraph, *First, it is noted for the Wheaten River, which is very wide and beautiful, indeed* gives an answer to this question. That is, the second sentence gives some explanation for the fact that Wheaten is a famous town.

The second and third sentences are called supporting sentences. They are called "supporting" because they "support," or explain, the idea expressed in the topic sentence. At minimum, you should have at least five to seven sentences in your paragraph. Here we can see our paragraph about Wheaten with a few more supporting sentences in bold font:

> My hometown is famous for several amazing natural features. First, it is noted for the Wheaten River, which is very wide and beautiful. Also, on the other side of the town is Wheaten Hill, which is unusual because it is very steep. The third amazing feature is the Big Old Tree. This tree stands two hundred feet tall and is probably about six hundred years old.

Details in Paragraphs

The short paragraph in this lesson is a fairly complete paragraph, but it lacks details. Whenever possible, you should include enough details in your paragraphs to help your reader understand exactly what you are writing about. In the paragraph about Wheaten, three natural landmarks are mentioned, but we do not know very much about them. Consider this revision:

> My hometown is famous for several amazing natural features. First, it is noted for the Wheaten River, which is very wide and beautiful. On either side of this river, which is 175 feet wide, are many willow trees which have long branches that can move gracefully in the wind. In autumn the leaves of these trees fall and cover the river banks like golden snow. Also, on the other side of the town is Wheaten Hill, which is unusual because it is very steep. Even though it is steep, climbing this hill is not dangerous, because there are some firm rocks along the sides that can be used as stairs. There are no trees around this hill, so it stands clearly against the sky and can be seen from many miles away. The third amazing feature is the Big Old Tree. This tree stands two hundred feet tall and is probably about six hundred years old. These three landmarks are truly amazing and make my hometown a famous place.

Why are details important? Consider the example of the hamburger, mentioned above. If the hamburger buns are the topic and concluding sentences, then the meat, the cheese, the lettuce, and so on are the supporting details. Without the food between the hamburger buns, your hamburger would not be very delicious! Similarly, without supporting details, your paragraph would not be very interesting.

A Note on Formality. In addition to having a particular kind of structure, academic paragraphs are different from "ordinary writing" in that certain kinds of expressions are not allowed.

Also, in formal essays you should avoid the first and second person. That is, do not use the pronouns *I* or *you*. The pronouns *we* and *us* are sometimes used in formal essays in some major fields, but in general you should not use these unless you are certain that they are customary in your field and/or your professor allows them. It is safer simply to use the third person.

TOO INFORMAL(Do not use)	ACCEPTABLE
don't	do not
doesn't	does not
aren't	are not
weren't	were not
can't	cannot
couldn't	could not
won't	will not

Coherence refers to a certain characteristic or aspect of writing. Literally, the word means "to stick together." Coherence in writing means that all the ideas in a paragraph flow smoothly from one sentence to the next sentence.

Major Connectors

Look at the words in bold font. Do you see how they help guide the reader? For example, consider the words, First, Second, and The third amazing feature. We can call these words *major connectors.* Major connectors help organise the main parts of your paragraph. This paragraph has three main parts: (1) a part about the Wheaten River, (2) a part about Wheaten Hill, and (3) a part about the Big Old Tree. Another way of saying this is that this paragraph has three main points which are indicated by the major connectors.

Minor Connectors

What about the other words in bold, such as those appearing in the phrases "these trees" and "this hill"? We can call these *minor connectors.* Minor connectors provide coherence to a paragraph by connecting sentences *within* each of the main parts of your paragraph. That is, when you write about your main points, you can use minor connectors to link your details to each main point. Now, look at this paragraph. Can you identify the main points?

> Each of the U.S. Manned space exploration projects had specific major goals. The Mercury project was designed to test whether or not human beings could survive and function in outer space. The Mercury project tested rockets with the new Mercury space capsule, which could hold one person. The Gemini project was intended to find out whether two people could work in the weightless environment of space. Gemini astronauts took "spacewalks." They floated outside their spacecraft in a spacesuit, connected to it by a tether. Gemini astronauts tried out new flying skills. Some astronauts flew two spacecraft extremely close together; this procedure was called "rendezvous." On some Gemini flights, astronauts physically linked two spacecraft together. Linking, or "space docking," was a major goal of the Gemini program. The Apollo project, with three astronauts, was intended to test spacecraft and skills so that people could actually fly to the Moon and land on it. Performing scientific experiments on the lunar surface and collecting rocks for study on Earth were goals.

Was this paragraph a little confusing to read? Now consider the same paragraph with a few changes:

> Each of the U.S. Manned space exploration projects had specific major goals. For example, the Mercury project was designed to test whether or not human beings could survive and function in outer space. *In addition,* the Mercury project tested rockets with the new Mercury space capsule, which could hold one person. As another example, the Gemini project was intended to find out whether two people could work in the weightless environment of space. *One way of doing this* was by having Gemini astronauts take "spacewalks." *That is,* they floated outside their spacecraft in a spacesuit, connected to it by a tether. Gemini astronauts *allosteric* out new flying skills. *For example,* some astronauts flew two spacecraft extremely close together; this procedure was called "rendezvous." On some Gemini

> flights, astronauts physically linked two spacecraft together. *This linking,* or "space docking," was a major goal of the Gemini program. Finally, the Apollo project, with three astronauts, had the goal of testing spacecraft and skills so that people could actually fly to the Moon and land on it. *Other goals included* performing scientific experiments on the lunar surface and collecting rocks for study on Earth.

Do you see which of the connectors above are major and which are minor? The major ones are in the second sentence, which introduces the first supporting point; *As another example,* which begins the second main point; and the word *Finally,* which introduces the third and last main point.

As for the minor connectors, we can divide them into three groups. The first group of minor connectors provides coherence for the first main point. There is only one minor connector in this first group, *In addition,* although it is possible to have more than one, depending on how many details you have to support your first main point.

The second group of minor connectors consists of *That is, also,* and also the phrase *For example* in the sentence, "For example, some astronauts..." Notice that this last minor connector is the same as the major connector at the beginning of the paragraph.

The third group of minor connectors in this particular paragraph also has one member, which is *Other goals included.*

Here is a table of a few common connectors

For example,	As another example,	On the one
For instance,	Another example of [xxx]	hand,
One example of	is (that)	On the other
(this) is	Finally,	hand,
First, Second,	In conclusion,	However,
Third, etc.	To summarise,	..., but...
	Also	

Paragraph Unity

Unity is a very important characteristic of good paragraph writing. Paragraph unity means that one paragraph is about ONLY ONE main topic. That is, all the sentences — the topic, supporting sentences, the detail sentences, and the concluding sentence — are all telling the reader about ONE main topic. If your paragraph contains a sentence or some sentences that are NOT related to the main topic, then we say that the paragraph "lacks unity," or that the sentence is "off-topic."

Look at the following paragraph, which is similar to the paragraph that we have studied above. Does it have perfect unity? Try to find the sentence that is off-topic:

> Each of the Russian manned space exploration projects had specific major goals. For example, the Vostok project was designed to test whether or not human beings could survive and function in outer space. For another example, the Voshk hod project was intended to find out whether people could work in the weightless environment of space. One Voshk hod cosmonaut experimented with weightlessness by taking a "spacewalk." That is, he floated in a spacesuit outside his Voshk hod spacecraft, connected to it by a tether. The cosmonaut to do this was Alexei Leonov. Several weeks later, Leonov's spacewalk was followed by that of U.S. astronaut Ed White. Finally, the Soyuz project, with three cosmonauts, had goals of testing spacecraft and space flight skills so that people could fly long missions in Earth orbit.

This paragraph is generally good, but the sentence, *Several weeks later, Leonov's spacewalk was followed by that of U.S. Astronaut Ed White,* does not have anything to do with the major goals of the various Russian space projects. In order to improve the paragraph, we should omit this sentence, even though it is historically accurate.

Knowing how to organise your ideas in such long essays is very important for academic success. Generally, academic essays have a similar format. They are at least five paragraphs long, although often they are much longer. Also, the basic structure of each of these paragraphs is the same as that which we have already studied. In addition, the paragraphs in the U.S. Academic essay can be divided into three basic kinds: (1) the introductory paragraph, (2) the body paragraphs, and (3) the concluding paragraph.

The Introduction

The first paragraph of the academic essay is the one that is usually the most different from the basic paragraph that we have studied. A basic paragraph had a topic sentence as its first sentence, followed by supporting sentences with supporting details, and these followed by a concluding sentence.

In the multi-paragraph academic essay, however, the structure is a little different. Like the basic paragraph, the introductory paragraph opens with a very general statement about the topic, and is often followed by some supporting examples, but the paragraph then finishes with a narrow statement about the topic. This narrow statement is called the main thesis.

The Body

The body portion of the essay is the largest portion. Typically, it has three paragraphs, but it might have two paragraphs and of course it can have many more than three. Each of these paragraphs usually has a topic sentence and several supporting sentences, just like the basic paragraph we have studied.

Recall that the main thesis statement of this essay said, *Similarly, the ocean of outer space has many dangers, but it also has several unique challenges for explorers.* You can see how the body of the essay is organised according to the challenges that are mentioned in the main thesis. The first body paragraph discusses the dangers of space vacuum, the second body paragraph gives information about meteors, and the third paragraph mentions the fact that water is very difficult to find on other planets.

Conclusion

In formal paragraphs you will sometimes see a sentence at the end of the paragraph which summarizes the information that has been presented. This is the concluding sentence. You can think of a concluding sentence as a sort of topic sentence in reverse.

You can understand concluding sentences with this example. Consider a hamburger that you can buy at a fast-food restaurant. A hamburger has a top bun meat, cheese, lettuce, and other elements in the middle of the hamburger, and a bottom bun. Note how the top bun and the bottom bun are very similar. The top bun, in a way, is like a topic sentence, and the bottom bun is like the concluding sentence. Similarly, the topic sentence and concluding sentence "hold" the supporting sentences in the paragraph.

5

Style of Writing

Style may be defined as the peculiar manner in which a man expresses his conceptions through the medium of language. It depends upon the choice of words and their arrangement to convey a meaning. Scarcely any two writers have exactly the same style, that is to say, express their ideas after the same peculiar form, just as no two mortals are fashioned by nature in the same mould, so that one is an exact counterpart of the other. Just as men differ in the accent and tones of their voices, so do they differ in the construction of their language.

Two reporters sent out on the same mission, say to report a fire, will verbally differ in their accounts though materially both descriptions will be the same as far as the leading facts are concerned. One will express himself in a style *different* from the other.

If you are asked to describe the dancing of a red-haired lady at the last charity ball you can either say–the ruby Circle, with the Titian locks glowing like the oriflamme which surrounds the golden god of day as he sinks to rest amid the crimson glory of the burnished West, gave a divine exhibition of the Terpsichorean art which thrilled the souls of the multitude" or, you can simply say– "The red-haired lady danced very well and pleased the audience."

The former is a specimen of the ultra florid or bombastic style which may be said to depend upon the pomposity of verbosity for its effect, the latter is a specimen of simple *natural* Style. Needless to say it is to be preferred. The other should be avoided. It stamps the writer as a person of shallowness, ignorance and inexperience. It has been eliminated from the newspapers. Even the most flatulent of yellow sheets no longer tolerate it in their columns. Affectation and pedantry in style are now universally condemned.

It is the duty of every speaker and writer to labour after a pleasing style. It gains him an entrance where he would otherwise be debarred. Often the interest of a subject depends as much on the way it is presented as on the subject itself. One writer will make it attractive, another repulsive. For instance take a passage in history. Treated by one historian it is like a desiccated mummy, dry, dull, disgusting, while under the spell of another it is, as it were, galvanised into a virile living thing which not only pleases but captivates the reader.

Requisite of Style

Diction

The first requisite of style is *choice* of *words*, and this comes under the head of *Diction*, the property of style which has reference to the words and phrases used in speaking and writing. The secret of literary skill from any standpoint consists in putting the right word in the right place. In order to do this it is imperative to know the meaning of the words we use, their exact literal meaning. Many synonymous words are seemingly interchangeable and appear as if the same meaning were applicable to three or four of them at the same time, but when all such words are reduced to a final analysis it is clearly seen that there is a marked difference in their meaning. For instance *grief* and *sorrow* seem to be identical, but they are not. *Grief* is active, *sorrow* is more or less passive; *grief* is caused by troubles and misfortunes which come to us from the outside, while *sorrow* is often the consequence of our own acts. *Grief* is frequently loud and violent, *sorrow* is always quiet and retiring. *Grief* shouts, *Sorrow* remains calm.

If you are not sure of the exact meaning of a word look it up immediately in the dictionary. Sometimes some of our great scholars are puzzled over simple words in regard to meaning, spelling or pronunciation. Whenever you meet a strange word note it down until you discover its meaning and use. Read the best books you can get, books written by men and women who are acknowledged masters of language, and study how they use their words, where they place them in the sentences, and the meanings they convey to the readers.

Mix in good society. Listen attentively to good talkers and try to imitate their manner of expression. If a word is used you do not understand, don't be ashamed to ask its meaning.

True, a small vocabulary will carry you through, but it is an advantage to have a large one. When you live alone a little pot serves just as well as a large one to cook your victuals and it is handy and convenient, but when your friends or neighbours come to dine with you, you will need a much larger pot and it is better to have it in store, so that you will not be put to shame for your scantiness of furnishings.

Get as many words as you possibly can–if you don't need them now, pack them away in the garrets of your brain so that you can call upon them if you require them. Keep a note book, jot down the words you don't understand or clearly understand and consult the dictionary when you get time.

Purity

Purity of style consists in using words which are reputable, national and present, which means that the words are in current use by the best authorities, that they are used throughout the nation and not confined to one particular part, and that they are words in constant use at the present time. There are two guiding principles in the choice of words–good use and good taste. Good use tells us whether a word is right or wrong; good taste, whether it is adapted to our purpose or not.

A word that is obsolete or too new to have gained a place in the language, or that is a provincialism, should not be used. Here are the ten commandments of English style:

1. Do not use foreign words.
2. Do not use a long word when a short one will serve your purpose. *Fire* is much better than *conflagration*.
3. Do not use technical words, or those understood only by specialists in their respective lines, except when you are writing especially for such people.
4. Do not use slang.
5. Do not use provincialisms, as "I guess" for "I think"; "I reckon" for "I know," etc.

6. Do not in writing prose, use poetical or antiquated words: as "lore, e'er, born, yea, nay, verily, peradventure."
7. Do not use trite and hackneyed words and expressions; as, "on the job," "up and in"; "down and out."
8. Do not use newspaper words which have not established a place in the language as "to bugle"; "to suicide," etc.
9. Do not use ungrammatical words and forms; as, "I am't;" "he don't."
10. Do not use ambiguous words or phrases; as– "He showed me all about the house."

Trite words, similes and metaphors which have become hackneyed and worn out should be allowed to rest in the oblivion of past usage. Such expressions and phrases as "Sweet sixteen" "the Almighty Money," "Uncle Sam," "On the fence," "The Glorious Fourth," "Young America," "The lords of creation," "The rising generation," "The weaker sex," "The weaker vessel," "Sweetness long drawn out" and "chief cook and bottle washer," should be put on the shelf as they are utterly worn out from too much usage.

Some of the old similes which have outlived their usefulness and should be pensioned off, are "Sweet as sugar," "Bold as a lion," "Strong as an ox," "Quick as a flash," "Cold as ice," "Stiff as a poker," "White as snow," "Busy as a bee," "Pale as a ghost," "Rich as Croesus," "Cross as a bear" and a great many more far too numerous to mention.

Be as original as possible in the use of expression. Don't follow in the old rut but try and strike out for yourself. This does not mean that you should try to set the style, or do anything outlandish or out of the way, or be an innovator on the prevailing custom. In order to be original there is no necessity for you to introduce something novel or establish a precedent.

The probability is you are not fit to do either, by education or talent. While following the style of those who are acknowledged leaders you can be original in your language. Try and clothe an idea different from what it has been clothed and better. If you are speaking or writing of dancing don't talk or write about "tripping the light fantastic toe." It is over two hundred years since Milton expressed it that way in 'L'Allegro." You're not a Milton and besides over a million have stolen it from Milton until it is now no longer worth stealing.

Don't resurrect obsolete words such as *whilom*, *yclept*, *wis*, etc., and be careful in regard to obsolescent words, that is, words that are at the present time gradually passing from use such as *quoth, trow, betwixt, amongst, froward*, etc.

Beware of new words. Be original in the construction and arrangement of your language, but don't try to originate words. Leave that to the Masters of language, and don't be the first to try such words, wait until the chemists of speech have tested them and passed upon their merits.

Propriety

Propriety of style consists in using words in their proper sense and as in the case of purity, good usage is the principal test. Many words have acquired in actual use a meaning very different from what they once possessed. "Prevent" formerly meant to go before, and that meaning is implied in its Latin derivation. Now it means to put a stop to, to hinder. To attain propriety of style it is necessary to avoid confounding words derived from the same root; as *respectfully* and *respectively*; it is necessary to use words in their accepted sense or the sense which everyday use sanctions.

Simplicity

Simplicity of style has reference to the choice of simple words and their unaffected presentation. Simple words should always be used in preference to compound, and complicated ones when they express the same or almost the same meaning. The Anglo-Saxon element in our language comprises the simple words which express the relations of everyday life, strong, terse, vigorous, the language of the fireside, street, market and farm. It is this style which characterises the Bible and many of the great English classics such as the "Pilgrim's Progress," "Robinson Crusoe," and "Gulliver's Travels."

Clearness

Clearness of style should be one of the leading considerations with the beginner in composition. He must avoid all obscurity and ambiguous phrases. If he write a sentence or phrase and see that a meaning might be inferred from it otherwise than intended, he should re-write it in such a way that there can be no possible doubt. Words, phrases or clauses that are closely related should be placed as near to each other as possible that their mutual relation may clearly appear, and no word should be omitted that is necessary to the complete expression of thought.

Unity

Unity is that property of style which keeps all parts of a sentence in connection with the principal thought and logically subordinate to it. A sentence may be constructed as to suggest the idea of oneness to the mind, or it may be so loosely put together as to produce a confused and indefinite impression. Ideas that have but little connection should be expressed in separate sentences, and not crowded into one. Keep long parentheses out of the middle of your sentences and when you have apparently brought your sentences to a close don't try to continue the thought or idea by adding supplementary clauses.

Strength

Strength is that property of style which gives animation, energy and vivacity to language and sustains the interest of the reader. It is as necessary to language as good food is to the body. Without it the words are weak and feeble and create little or no impression on the mind. In order to have strength the language must be concise, that is, much expressed in little compass, you must hit the nail fairly on the head and drive it in straight. Go critically over what you write and strike out every word, phrase and clause the omission of which impairs neither the clearness nor force of the sentence and so avoid redundancy, tautology and circumlocution. Give the most important words the most prominent places, which, as has been pointed out elsewhere, are the beginning and end of the sentence.

Harmony

Harmony is that property of style which gives a smoothness to the sentence, so that when the words are sounded their connection becomes pleasing to the ear. It adapts sound to sense. Most people construct their sentences without giving thought to the way they will sound and as a consequence we have many jarring and discordant combinations such as "Thou strengthenedst thy position and actedst arbitrarily and derogatorily to my interests."

Harsh, disagreeable verbs are liable to occur with the Quaker form *Thou* of the personal pronoun. This form is now nearly obsolete, the plural *you* being almost universally used. To obtain harmony in the sentence long words that are hard to pronounce and combinations of letters of one kind should be avoided.

Expressivenes

Style is expressive of the writer, as to who he is and what he is. As a matter of structure in composition it is the indication of what a man can do; as a matter of quality it is an indication of what he is.

Kinds of Style

Style has been classified in different ways, but it admits of so many designations that it is very hard to enumerate a table. In fact there are as many styles as there are writers, for no two authors write *exactly after* the same form. However, we may classify the styles of the various authors in broad divisions as *(a)* dry, *(b)* plain, *(c)* neat, *(d)* elegant, *(e)* florid, *(f)* bombastic.

The *dry* style excludes all ornament and makes no effort to appeal to any sense of beauty. Its object is simply to express the thoughts in a correct manner. This style is exemplified by Berkeley.

The *plain* style does not seek ornamentation either, but aims to make clear and concise statements without any elaboration or embellishment. Locke and Whately illustrate the plain style.

The *neat* style only aspires after ornament sparingly. Its object is to have correct figures, pure diction and clear and harmonious sentences. Goldsmith and Gray are the acknowledged leaders in this kind of style.

The *elegant* style uses every ornament that can beautify and avoids every excess which would degrade. Macaulay and Addison have been enthroned as the kings of this style. To them all writers bend the knee in homage.

The *florid* style goes to excess in superfluous and superficial ornamentation and strains after a highly coloured imagery. The poems of Ossian typify this style.

The *bombastic* is characterised by such an excess of words, figures and ornaments as to be ridiculous and disgusting. It is like a circus clown dressed up in gold tinsel Dickens gives a fine example of it in Sergeant Buzfuz' speech in the "Pickwick Papers." Among other varieties of style may be mentioned the colloquial, the laconic, the concise, the diffuse, the abrupt the flowing, the quaint, the epigrammatic, the flowery, the feeble, the nervous, the vehement, and the affected. The manner of these is sufficiently indicated by the adjective used to describe them.

In fact, style is as various as character and expresses the individuality of the writer, or in other words, as the French writer Buffon very aptly remarks, "the style is the man himself."

Figures of Speech

Figures of speech is mode of expression in which words are used out of their literal meaning or out of their ordinary use in order to add beauty or emotional intensity or to transfer the poet's sense impressions by comparing or identifying one thing with another that has a meaning familiar to the reader. Some important figures of speech are: simile, metaphor, personification, hyperbole and symbol.

We use figures of speech in "figurative language" to add colour and interest, and to awaken the imagination. Figurative language is everywhere, from classical works like Shakespeare or the Bible, to everyday speech, pop music and television commercials. It makes the reader or listener use their imagination and understand much more than the plain words.

Figurative language is the opposite of literal language. Literal language means exactly what it says. Figurative language means something different to (and usually more than) what it says on the surface:

— He ran fast. (literal)

— He ran like the wind. (Figurative)

In the above example "like the wind" is a figure of speech (in this case, a simile). It is important to recognise the difference between literal and figurative language. There are many figures of speech that are commonly used and which you can learn by heart. At other times, writers and speakers may invent their own figures of speech. If you do not recognise them as figures of speech and think that they are literal, you will find it difficult to understand the language.

As figurative language is to be met with in almost every sentence; and, when properly employed, confers beauty and strength on composition; some knowledge of it appears to be indispensable to the scholars, who are learning to form their sentences with perspicuity, accuracy, and force. We shall, therefore, enumerate the principal figures, and give them some explanation.

In general, Figures of Speech imply some departure from simplicity of expression; the idea which we mean to convey is expressed in a particular manner, and with some circumstance added, which is designed to render the impression more strong and vivid. When I say, for instance, "That a good man enjoys comfort in the midst of adversity"; I just express my thoughts in the simplest manner possible: but when I say, "To the upright there arise the light in darkness"; the same sentiment is expressed in a figurative style; a new circumstance is introduced; "light," is put in the place of "comfort," and "darkness" is used to suggest the idea of "adversity."...

But, though figures imply a deviation from what may be reckoned the most simple form of speech, we are not thence to conclude, that they imply anything uncommon, or unnatural. On many occasions, they are both the most natural, and the most common method of uttering our sentiments. It would be very difficult to compose any discourse without using them often; nay, there are few sentences of considerable length, in which there does not occur some expression that may be termed a figure. This being the case, we may see the necessity of some attention, in order to understand their nature and use.

At the first rise of language, men would begin with giving names to the different objects which they discerned, or thought of. The stock of words would, then, be very small. As men's ideas multiplied, and their acquaintance with objects increased, their store of names and words would also increase. But to the vast variety of objects and ideas, no language is adequate. No language is so copious, as to have a separate word for every separate idea.

Men naturally sought to abridge this labour of multiplying words without end; and, in order to lay less burden on their memories, made one word, which they had already appropriated to a certain idea or object, stand also for some other idea or object, between which and the primary one, they found, or fancied, some relation. The names of sensible objects, were the words most early introduced; and were, by degrees, extended to those mental objects, of which men had more obscure conceptions, and to which they found it more difficult to assign distinct names. They borrowed, therefore, the name of some sensible idea, where their imagination found some affinity. Thus, we speak of a piercing judgment, and a clear head; a soft or a hard heart; a rough or smooth behaviour. We say, inflamed by anger, warmed by love, swelled with pride, melted into grief; and these are almost the only significant words which we have for such ideas.

Figures make speech more effective, they beautify and emphasise it and give to it a relish and piquancy as salt does to food; besides they add energy and force to expression so that it irresistibly compels attention and interest. There are four kinds of figures, viz.:

1. *Figures of orthography* which change the spelling of a word;
2. *Figures of etymology* which change the form of words;
3. *Figures of Syntax* which change the construction of sentences;
4. *Figures of Rhetoric* or the art of speaking and writing effectively which change the mode of thought.

We shall only consider the last mentioned here as they are the most important, really giving to language the construction and style which make it a fitting medium for the intercommunication of ideas. Figures of Rhetoric have been variously classified, some authorities extending the list to a useless length. The fact is that any form of expression which conveys thought may be classified as a Figure.

The principal figures as well as the most important and those oftenest used are, Simile, Metaphor, Personification, Allegory, Synecdoche, Metonymy, Exclamation, Hyperbole, Apostrophe,

Vision, Antithesis, Climax, Epigram, Interrogation and Irony. The first four are founded on resemblance, the second six on contiguity and the third five, on contrast.

Simile

A simile is a figure of speech that says that one thing is like another different thing. We can use similes to make descriptions more emphatic or vivid.

We often use the words as says and like with similes.

Common patterns for similes, with example sentences, are:

— something [is*] AS adjective AS something

His skin was as cold as ice.

It felt as hard as rock.

She looked as gentle as a lamb.

— Something [is*] like something

My love is like a red, rose.

These cookies taste like garbage.

He had a temper (that was) like a volcano.

— Something [does**] like something

He eats like a pig.

He smokes like a chimney.

They fought like cats and dogs.

* *sedative verb: be, feel, smell, taste etc*

** *action verb*

Here are some more examples of well known similes:

[is] AS adjective AS something	*Meaning*
as blind as a bat	completely blind
as cold as ice	very cold
as flat as a pancake	completely flat
as gentle as a lamb	very gentle
as light as a feather	very light
as old as the hills	very old

as sharp as a knife	very sharp
as strong as a bull	very strong
as white as snow	pure white
as wise as an owl	very wise
[is] LIKE something	possible meaning (depending on context)
like a rose	beautiful
like a volcano	explosive
like garbage	disgusting
like an animal	inhuman
like spaghetti	entangled
like dewdrops	sweet and pure
like godliest	precious
like a tip	very untidy
like a dream	wonderful, incredible
like stars	bright and beautiful
[does] LIKE something	*meaning*
to drink like a fish	to drink a lot
to eat like a bird	to eat very little
to eat like a horse	to eat a lot
to eat like a pig	to eat impolitely
to fight like cats and dogs	to fight fiercely
to sing like an angel	to sing beautifully
to sleep like a log	to sleep well and soundly
to smoke like a chimney	to smoke heavily, all time
to soar like an eagle	to fly high and free
to work like a dog	to work very hard

Note that with the As says pattern, the first AS is sometimes suppressed, for example:

— His skin was cold as ice.

The above patterns of simile are the most common, but there are others made with adverbs or words such as than and as if, for example:

— He ran as fast as the wind.

— He is larger than life.

— They ran as if for their lives.

Similes can include other figures of speech. For example, "He ran like greased lightning" is a simile that includes hyperbole (greased lightning).

Similes often make use of irony or sarcasm. In such cases they may even mean the opposite of the adjective used. Look at these examples:

— His explanation was as clear as mud.

— The film was about as interesting as watching a copy of Windows down load.

Similes are often found (and they sometimes originate) in poetry and other literature. Here are a few examples:

— A woman without a man is like a fish without a bicycle—*Irina Dunn*

— Dawn breaks open like a wound that bleeds afresh—*Wilfred Owen*

— Death has many times invited me: it was like the salt invisible in the waves—*Pablo Neruda*

— Guiltless forever, like a tree—*Robert Browning*

— Happy as pigs in mud—*David Eddings*

— How like the winter hath my absence been— *William Shakespeare*

— As idle as a painted ship upon a painted ocean—*Samuel Taylor Coleridge*

— Jubilant as a flag unfurled—*Dorothy Parker*

Many similes are cliches. You should use well know similes with care, but it is certainly useful to know them so that you can understand language that contains them.

Metaphor

A metaphor is a figure of speech that says that one thing is another different thing. This allows us to use fewer words and forces the reader or listener to find the similarities. The word metaphor comes from the Greek word *metapherin* (meaning "transfer").

The simplest form of metaphor is: "The [first thing] is a [second thing." Look at this example:

— Her *home* was a *prison.*

In the above sentence, we understand immediately that her home had some of the characteristics of a prison. Mainly, we imagine, she could not leave her home. She was trapped inside. Why it was a prison we do not know, but that would be clear from the context—perhaps her husband forced her to stay at home, perhaps she was afraid of the outside. We don't know, but the rest of the story would tell us.

What is important here is that in five simple words we understand a lot about her environment, how she felt and how she behaved. In this sentence, "prison" is a metaphor. Look at another example:

— *Pinky* is a *sheep.*

What is one characteristic of sheep? They follow each other. So we can imagine that Pinky is a follower, not a leader. In this sentence "sheep" is a metaphor.

Metaphors are very common in everyday language. But poets also like to use metaphors. In the following famous verse, can you spot three metaphors in the first three lines?

> The wind was a torrent of darkness among the gusty trees,
> The moon was a ghostly galleon tossed upon cloudy seas,
> The road was a ribbon of moonlight over the purple moor,
> And the highwayman came riding—
> —riding—
> The highwayman came riding, up to the old inn-door.

Look at the examples of metaphors given in table of next page with sample sentences and meanings. All these metaphors are nouns. But there are other ways of making metaphors, for example with verbs or adjectives.

Difference Between Metaphor and Simile

Both similes and metaphors link one thing to another. A simile usually uses "as" or "like". A metaphor is a condensed simile, a short-cut to meaning, which omits "as" or "like." A metaphor creates a relationship directly and leaves more to the imagination. With simile A is *like* B. With metaphor A *is* B.

Simile	*Metaphor*
Your eyes are like the sun.	You are my sunshine.
He eats like a pig.	He is a pig.
He lives like a pig.	

In the phrase "to grasp the concept" the physical action "to grasp" is used as a metaphor for "to understand" (which is non-physical). But this phrase has been used so often that most English speakers do not have an image of the physical action in their mind. This metaphor has died; it is a "dead metaphor".

The awkward use of two or more different metaphors at the same time is normally best avoided. It creates conflicting images in the reader or listener's mind, reduces each metaphor's impact, and generally causes confusion. Look at this example:

— America is a *melting pot* where new ideas are *kindled.*

Hyperbole

Hyperbole is a figure of speech that uses an exaggerated or extravagant statement to create a strong emotional response. As a figure of speech it is not intended to be taken literally. Hyperbole is frequently used for humour. Examples of hyperbole are:

— They ran like greased lightning.

— He's got tons of money.

— Her brain is the size of a pea.

— He is older than the hills.

— I will die if she asks me to dance.

— She is as big as an elephant!

— I'm so hungry I could eat a horse.

— I have told you a million times not to lie!

The media and the advertising industry often use hyperbole (which may then be described as hype or media hype).

Oxymoron

An oxymoron is a figure of speech that deliberately uses two contradictory ideas. This contradiction creates a paradoxical image in the reader or listener's mind that generates a new concept or meaning for the whole. Some typical oxyneurine are:

— A living death.

— Sometimes you have to be cruel to be kind.

— A deafening silence.

— Bitter-sweet.

— The Sounds of Silence (song title).

— Make haste slowly.

— He was conspicuous by his absence.

Pseudo Oxyneurine

In the standard meaning of oxymoron the contradiction is deliberate. However, in popular usage oxymoron is sometimes used to mean "contradiction in terms", where the contradiction is unintentional. Such expressions, unlike real oxymorons, are commonly used without any sense of paradox in everyday language, for example:

— Anecdotal evidence.

— Friendly fire.

— Pretty ugly.

A common attempt at humour is to describe a certain phrase as an oxymoron, implying that the two parts of the phrase are mutually exclusive and that consequently the phrase as a whole must be nonsensical:

— Airline food.

— India culture.

— Eco-Tourism.

— Computer security.

— Military intelligence.

Personification

Personification (from the Latin *persona*, person, and *facer*, to make) is the treating of an inanimate object as if it were animate and is probably the most beautiful and effective of all the figures.

> "The mountains sing together, the hills rejoice and clap their hands."
>
> "Earth felt the wound; and Nature from her seat, Sighing, through all her works, gave signs of woe."

Personification is the treating of an inanimate object as if it were animate and is probably the most beautiful and effective of all the figures of speech. Personification depends much on a vivid imagination and is adapted especially to poetical composition. It has two distinguishable forms:

- When personality is ascribed to the inanimate as in "The mountains sing together, the hills rejoice and clap their hands."
- When some quality of life is attributed to the inanimate; as, a raging storm; an angry sea; a whistling wind, etc.

Poems with personification examples can be found by the most famous poets including John Milton and Robert Frost.

- "Confusion heards his voice." from *Paradise Lost*— Book 3 by John Milton.
- Another example of personification from *Paradise Lost* by John Milton "Earth felt the wound; and Nature from her seat, Sighing, through all her works, gave signs of woe."
- *Spring Pools* by Robert Frost "And like the flowers beside them chill and shiver, Will like the flowers beside them soon be gone."

Examples of personification can be found in many examples of the poem, poems or poetry. Famous poets use this figure of speech to convey and emphasise unusual and vivid images. The use of strong word association changes the mode of thought and adds variation, embellishment and adornment to literary works.

In figurative language we use words in such a way that they differ somewhat from ordinary everyday speech and convey meanings in a more vivid and impressive manner. Figures, like personification make speech more effective, they beautify and emphasise it in Rhetoric which is the art of speaking and writing effectively. Figures of speech such as Personification use word association to convey emotion and mood often in a non-literal sense.

Figures of speech such as personification adds adornment, beautifies, colours, elegant variation, embellishment, embroidery, emphasis, exaggeration, exclamation, flourish, floweriness, irony, lushness and luxuriance to the English language.

Allegory

An Allegory, is a form of expression in which the words are symbolical of something. It is very closely allied to the metaphor, in fact is a continued metaphor. Allegory, metaphor and simile have three points in common,—they are all founded on resemblance. "Ireland is like a thorn in the side of England;" this is simile. "Ireland is a thorn in the side of England;" this is metaphor. "Once a great giant sprang up out of the sea and lived on an island all by himself.

On looking around he discovered a little girl on another small island near by. He thought the little girl could be useful to him in many ways so he determined to make her subservient to his will. He commanded her, but she refused to obey, then he resorted to very harsh measures with the little girl, but she still remained obstinate and obdurate. He continued to oppress her until finally she rebelled and became as a thorn in his side to prick him for his evil attitude towards her;" this is an allegory in which the giant plainly represents England and the little girl, Ireland; the implication is manifest though no mention is made of either country.

Strange to say the most perfect allegory in the English language was written by an almost illiterate and ignorant man, and written too, in a dungeon cell. In the "Pilgrim's Progress," Bunyan, the itinerant tinker, has given us by far the best allegory ever penned. Another good one is "The Feriae Queen" by Edmund Spencer.

Synecdoche

Synecdoche is a figure of speech in which:

— A term denoting a part of something is used to refer to the whole thing (Pars pro toto), or

— A term denoting a thing (a "whole") is used to refer to part of it (Totem pro parte), or

— A term denoting a specific class of thing is used to refer to a larger, more general class, or

— A term denoting a general class of thing is used to refer to a smaller, more specific class (Bindo pro parte), or

— A term denoting a material is used to refer to an object composed of that material.

In figurative language we use words in such a way that they differ somewhat from ordinary everyday speech and convey meanings in a more vivid and impressive manner. Figures, like synecdoche make speech more effective, they beautify and emphasise it in Rhetoric which is the art of speaking and writing effectively. Figures of speech such as synecdoche use word association to convey emotion and mood often in a non-literal sense.

Synecdoche is closely related to metonymy (the figure of speech in which a term denoting one thing is used to refer to a related thing); indeed, synecdoche is sometimes considered a subclass of metonymy. It is more distantly related to other figures of speech, such as metaphor.

Examples of synecdoche can be found in many examples of the poem, poems or poetry. Famous poets use this figure of speech to convey and emphasise unusual and vivid images. The use of strong word association changes the mode of thought and adds variation, embellishment and adornment to literary works.

Poems with synecdoche examples can be found by the most famous poets including Shakespeare, Swift and Frost:

— "Friends, Romans, countrymen: lend me your ears"—*One of the most famous example of synecdoche by William Shakespeare.*

— "Prepared to scrub the entry and the stairs. The youth with barmy stumps began to trace"—*From 'A Description of the Morning' by Jonathan Swift (1667-1745) where the stump of the broom's straw stands in for the whole of the broom.*

— Stopping by Woods on a Snowy Evening—*by Robert Frost where the journey through woods and forests in the poem represent life's journey.*

Metonymy

Metonymy is the designation of an object by one of its accompaniments, in other words, it is a figure by which the name of one object is put for another when the two are so related that the mention of one readily suggests the other. Thus when we say of a drunkard–"He loves the bottle" we do not mean that he loves the glass receptacle, but the liquor that it is supposed to contain. Metonymy, generally speaking, has, three subdivisions:

1. When an effect is put for cause or vice versa: as 'Gray hairs should be respected," meaning old age. "He writes a fine hand," that is, handwriting.
2. When the sign is put for the thing signified; as, "The pen is mightier than the sword," meaning literary power is superior to military force.
3. When the container is put for the thing contained; as "The House was called to order," meaning the members in the House.

Examples of metonymy can be found in many examples of literature or poetry. The use of strong word association changes the mode of thought and adds variation, embellishment and adornment to literary works.

In figurative language we use words in such a way that they differ somewhat from ordinary everyday speech and convey meanings in a more vivid and impressive manner. Figures, like metonymy make speech more effective, they beautify and emphasise it in rhetoric which is the art of speaking and writing effectively. Figures of speech such as metonymy use word association to convey emotion and mood often in a non-literal sense.

Figures of speech such as metonymy adds adornment, beautifies, colours, elegant variation, embellishment, embroidery, emphasis, exaggeration, exclamation, flourish, floweriness, irony, lushness and luxuriance to the English language.

Poems with metonymy examples can be found as follows:

— "He writes a fine hand" meaning good handwriting.

— "The pen is mightier than the sword," meaning literary power is superior to military force.

— "The House was called to order," meaning the members in the House.
— "We have always remained loyal to the crown."
— "He is a man of the cloth."
— "By the sweat of thy brow thou shalt eat thy bread."

Exclamation

Exclamation is a figure by which the speaker instead of stating a fact, simply utters an expression of surprise or emotion. For instance when he hears some harrowing tale of woe or misfortune instead of saying,– "It is a sad story" he exclaims "What a sad story!"

Exclamation may be defined as the vocal expression of feeling, though it is also applied to written forms which are intended to express emotion. Thus in describing a towering mountain we can write "Heavens, what a piece of Nature's handiwork! how majestic! how sublime! how awe-inspiring in its colossal impressive-ness!" This figure rather belongs to poetry and animated oratory than to the cold prose of everyday conversation and writing.

Apostrophe

Apostrophe is an exclamatory rhetorical figure of speech is an exclamatory rhetorical figure of speech, when a talker or writer breaks off and directs speech to an imaginary person or abstract quality or idea. In dramatic works and poetry written in or translated into English, such a figure of speech is often introduced by the exclamation "O".

It is related to personification, although in apostrophe, objects or abstractions are implied to have certain human qualities (such as understanding) by the very fact that the speaker is addressing them as he would a person in his presence.

Apostrophe is often used to convey extreme emotion, as in Claudius's impassioned speech in Hamlet.

Examples:

— "Where, O death, thy sting? Where, O death, thy victory?" 1 Corinthians 15:55, traditionally attributed to Saint Paul.

— "O Romeo, wherefore art thou Romeo?" Shakespeare, *Romeo and Juliet*, Act II, Scene 2

— "O, pardon me, thou bleeding piece of earth, / That I am meek and gentle with these butchers! / Thou art the ruins of the noblest man / That ever lived in the tide of times." Shakespeare, *Julius Caesar*, Act 3, Scene 1

— "To what green altar, O mysterious priest, / Lead'st thou that heifer lowing at the skies, / And all her silken flanks with garlands rest?" John Keats, "Ode on a Grecian Urn"

— "O eloquent, just, and mighty Death!" Sir Walter Raleigh, *A Historie of the World*

— "Roll on thou dark and deep blue ocean." Lord Byron, "Childe Herald's Pilgrimage"

— "Science! True daughter of Old Time thou art!" Edgar Allan Poe, "To Science"

— Common usage as an opposition speaker at a political convention: "And I say to you, Mr. President, we do not want our children to grow up in a world where...(etc.)"

— *O Captain! My Captain!*, title of Walt Whitman's poem

Vision

Vision is another figure of speech, which is proper only in animated and warm composition. It is produced when, instead of relating something that is past, we use the present tense, and describe it as actually passing before our eyes. Thus Cicerone, in his fourth oration against Catiline: "I seem to myself to behold this city, the ornament of the earth, and the capital of all nations, suddenly involved in one conflagration. I see before me the slaughtered heaps of citizens, lying un buried in the midst of their ruined country. The furious countenance of Cethegus rises to my view, while with a savage joy, he is triumphing in your miseries." This manner of description supposes a sort of enthusiasm, which carries the person who describes, in some measure out of himself; and, when well executed, must needs, by the force of sympathy, impress the reader or hearer very strongly.

Antithesis

The next figure in order, is *Antithesis*. Comparison is founded on the resemblance; antithesis, on the contrast or opposition of two objects. Contrast has always the effect, to make each of the contrasted objects appear in the stronger light. White, for instance, never appears so bright as when it is opposed to black; and when both are viewed together. An author, in his defence of a friend against the charge of murder, expresses himself thus: "Can you believe that the person whom he scrubbed to slay, when he might have done so with full justice, in a convenient place, at a proper time, with secure impunity; he made no scruple to murder against justice, in an unfavourable place, at an unseasonable time, and at the risk of capital condemnation?" The following examples further illustrate this figure.

— Tho' deep, yet clear; tho' gentle, yet not dull;
Strong, without rage; without over flowing, full.

— "If you wish to enrich a person, study not to increase his stores, but to diminish his desires."

— "If you regulate your desires according to the standard of nature, you will never be poor; if according to the standard of opinion, you will never be rich."

Maxims

A *maxim*, or moral saying, very properly receives the form of the two last examples; both because it is supposed to be the fruit of meditation, and because it is designed to be engraving on the memory, which recalls it more easily by the help of such contrasted expressions. But where such sentences frequently succeed each other; where this becomes an author's favourite and prevailing manner of expressing himself, his style appears too much studied and laboured; it gives us the impression of an author attending more to his manner of saying things, than to the things themselves.

Interrogation

The un figured, literal use of interrogation, is to ask a question: but when men are strongly moved, whatever they would affirm or deny, with great earnestness, they naturally put in the form of a question, expressing thereby the strongest confidence of the truth of their own sentiment, and appealing to their hearers for the impossibility of the contrary....

Interrogation gives life and spirit to discourse. We see this in the animated, introductory speech of Cicerone against Catiline: "How long will you, Catiline, abuse our patience? Do you not perceive that your designs are discovered?" He might indeed have said; "You abuse our patience a long while. You must be sensible, that your designs are discovered." But it is easy to perceive, how much this latter mode of expression, falls short of the force and vehemence of the former.

Irony

Irony is expressing ourselves in a manner contrary to our thoughts, not with a view to deceive, but to add force to our observations. Persons may be reproved for their negligence, by saying; "You have taken great care indeed." Cicerone says of the person against whom he was pleading; "We have great reason to believe that the modest man would not ask him for his debt, when he pursues his life."

Ironical exhortation is a very agreeable kind of figure; which, after having set the inconveniences of a thing, in the clearest light, concludes with a feigned encouragement to pursue it. Such is that of Hoarse, when, having beautifully described the noise and tumultus of Rome, he adds ironically; "Go now, and study tuneful verse at Rome." The subjects of Irony are vices and follies of all kinds: and this mode of exposing them, is often more effectual than serious reasoning. The gravest persons have not declined the use of this figure, on proper occasions. The wise and virtuous Socrates made great use of it, in his endeavours to discountenance vicious and foolish practices.... Exclamations and Irony are sometimes united: as in Cicerone's oration for Bulbus, where he derides his accuser, by saying; " O excellent interpreter of the law! Master of antiquity! Corrector and meander of our constitution."

Amplification and Climax

The last figure of speech that we shall mention, is what writers call

Amplification or *Climax*. It consists in heightening all the circumstances of an object or action, which we desire to place in a strong light. Cicerone gives a lively instance of this figure, when he says; "It is a crime to put a Roman citizen in bonds; it is the height of guilt to scourge him; little less than parricide to put him to death: what name then shall I give to the act of crucifying him?"...

Let us look at an example of a beautiful climax, taken from the charge of a judge to the jury, in the case of a woman accused of murdering her own child. "Gentlemen, if one man had any how slain another; if an adversary had killed his opposer, or a woman occasioned the death of her enemy; even these criminals would have been capitally punished by the Cornelian law; but if this guiltless infant, that could make no enemy, had been murdered by its own nurse, what punishment would not then the mother have demanded? With what cries and exclamations would she have stunned your ears! What shall we say then, when a woman, guilty of homicide, a mother, of the murder of her innocent child, hath comprised all those misdeeds in one single crime? A crime, in its own nature, detestable; in a woman prodigious; in a mother, incredible; and perpetrated against one whose age called for compassion, whose near relation claimed affection, and whose innocence deserved the highest favour."

Rules of Using Figures of Speech

We have now finished what was proposed, concerning Perspicuity in single words and phrases, and the accurate construction of sentences. The former has been considered under the heads of Purity, Propriety, and Precision; and the latter, under those of Clearness, Unity, Strength, and the proper use of Figurative Language. Though many of those attentions which have been recommended, may appear minute, yet their effect upon writing and style, is much greater than might, at first, be imagined. A sentiment which is expressed in accurate language, and in a period, clearly, neatly, and well arranged, always makes a stronger impression on the mind, than one that is expressed inaccurately, or in a feeble or embarrassed manner. Every one feels this upon a comparison: and if the effect be sensible in one sentence, how much more in a whole discourse, or composition that is made up of such sentences?

The fundamental rule for writing with accuracy, and into which all others might be resolved, undoubtedly is, *to communicate, in correct language, and in the clearest and most natural order, the ideas which we mean to transfuse into the minds of others*. Such a selection and arrangement of words, as do most justice to the sense, and express it to most advantage, make an agreeable and strong impression. To these points have tended all the rules which have been given.

Advantages

The principal advantages of figures of speech, are the two following:

First, They enrich language and render it more copious. By their means, words and phrases are multiplied, for expressing all sorts of ideas; for describing even the minutest differences; the nicest shades and colours of thought; which no language could possibly do by proper words alone, without assistance from Troupes.

Secondly, They frequently give us a much clearer and more striking view of the principal object, than we could have, if it were expressed in simple terms, and divested of its accessory idea. By a well-chosen figure, even conviction is assisted, and the impression of a truth upon the mind, made more lively and forcible than it would otherwise be. We perceive this in the following illustration of Young: " When we dip too deep in pleasure, we always stir a sediment that renders it impure and noxious"; and in this instance: " A heart boiling with violent passions, will always send up infatuating fumes to the head." An image that presents so much congruity between a moral and a sensible idea, serves, like an argument from analogy, to enforce what the author asserts, and to induce belief.

6

Paragraph Writing

A paragraph usually contains a general idea in one sentence, and 4 - 5 supporting sentences which expand this idea by giving explanation, details and/or examples to support the main idea. Length can vary.

On the page, the paragraph is a solid block of writing (like this!) To start a new paragraph, you should leave a whole line and start at the beginning of the line after. You can indent - if handwriting (start about 2 cm from the left), but this is not necessary if you have left a line.

Paragraphs are used to separate main ideas. A new paragraph signals to the reader that a new idea is about to be discussed. The break between paragraphs gives the reader time to take in each idea.

The length of a paragraph varies. A paragraph with a length of five sentences is normally sufficient to expand on an idea. Anything more than this may be better organized into a separate paragraph. This ensures not more than one idea is covered in one paragraph. After all, the purpose of paragraphs is to separate ideas. A new paragraph means a new idea is being talked about.

A paragraph starts off with a topic sentence. This first sentence introduces the main idea of the paragraph. The sentences that follow the topic sentence discuss the idea. Some of the things the writer does here to expand on the idea include establishing the facts, providing details, and quoting examples. They must strictly be about the idea and not deviate to something else.

The last sentence in a paragraph is the concluding sentence of the paragraph. Use different words to restate the idea as introduced by the topic sentence in this concluding sentence – a summary of what has been discussed.

Elements of Paragraph

There are three main sorts of sentences that can be used in every paragraph. Introductory, body, and concluding paragraphs all contain topic sentences, followed by detail sentences, and terminated by concluding or transition sentences. Their exact form and content is largely dependant on the context in which they are used. There are, however, unique rules concerning the construction of paragraph sentences which ensure coherence and universality within academic writing as such.

Paragraph sentences can never be constructed with the help of abbreviated forms. They, just like every other type of academic writing, should be written in formal and objective language. Paragraph sentences must be well-constructed in order to render the validity of all arguments in a credible manner. Writers should, naturally, avoid first and second voice perspective.

Topic Sentence

Topic sentences are often incorrectly defined as the first sentences in a paragraph. Topic sentences, in fact, can be situated as the second or third sentence. Topic sentence is about introducing the main idea of a paragraph, not about chronology. It should discuss an idea only in generic terms without providing too many details.

Supporting Sentences

Supporting sentences are also called detail sentences and they constitute the body of the paragraph. They, naturally, provide support to the statement or idea expressed in the introductory sentence. They must contain details which help to elaborate on the thought comprised in the topic sentence. They can compare and contrast facts, introduce quotations, and paraphrase secondary sources. They should explore only limited amounts of material and lead toward the concluding or transition sentence.

Concluding Sentence

Writing concluding sentences is, probably, the least complicated task in writing a paragraph. Concluding sentences, so-called terminators, restate the idea of the topic sentence. If possible, they should summarise the paragraph in such a way so as to expose the relevance of supporting arguments in the context of the topic sentence. Writing concluding sentences is, of course, very different from writing transition sentences.

Transition Sentence

The purpose of any transition sentence is to show in what way the content of above paragraph will be elaborated on in the following paragraph. Optionally, it can announce the relevance of the above paragraph for the development of its follower. Finally, the transition sentence may serve as a catalyst between two or more ideas which should be discussed in close relation to one another.

Types of Paragraphs

In order to write coherent essays, students must first learn about the functions of various paragraphs. Most paragraphs will have several functions to fulfil at a time; it is important to know under what circumstances their functions can be conjoined. The following list contains explanations about the content and style of different paragraphs.

Narration Paragraph

Narration paragraphs are most distinctively used in fiction. As such, they will contain all necessary components of action development: protagonist, setting, goal, obstacle, climax and resolution. Writing a narration paragraph requires, consequently, sequential order and chronology. There are many descriptive elements included into the body of a narration paragraph but, if composed correctly, the paragraph will feature much more action than depiction.

Exposition Paragraph

Often times, this kind of a paragraph is used as a component of other types. It's created in order to clarify or explain a problem or a phenomenon. Writing exposition paragraphs requires strict focus on evidence and objective language. It can contain elements of comparison and contrast or cause and effect writing - both facilitate accurate exposition of its subject-matter.

Definition Paragraph

Definition paragraphs are used in order to explain the meaning, origin and function of things. They are used both in academic writing and in fiction. To write a definition paragraph, writers should concentrate on the role of its subject in the context of the whole essay and list comparisons as well as examples accordingly.

Classification Paragraph

Writing a classification paragraph takes a slightly varied approach. It should rely on both defining and comparing. Writers should classify the subject of the paragraph in a specific context providing comparisons to corresponding ideas. Classification can be performed on multiple levels – semantic (comparing different meanings of things), linguistic (using vocabulary to show contrast), and more.

Description Paragraph

Preferably, description paragraphs should concentrate on action (verbs), rather than sensations (adverbs and adjectives). Writers should assume the role of readers whose idea of the described events is, in entirety, constructed by the paragraph content. Description paragraphs should be detailed, clear, and render the represented reality chronologically.

Process Analysis Paragraph

It, usually, takes the form of a how-to paragraph which guides readers through a process or action to be performed. It's very concise and uses formal, non-descriptive vocabulary. It should be written in chronological order which accounts for subsequent actions.

Persuasion Paragraph

Persuasion paragraphs require exhortatory and dynamic language. They are aimed at persuading others into taking a particular action or adopting certain point of view. They should be devoid of descriptive content and, instead, rely on the imperative mode.

Organising a Paragraph

There are many different ways to organise a paragraph. The organisation you choose will depend on the controlling idea of the paragraph. Below are a few possibilities for organisation, with brief examples.

— *Narration:* Tell a story. Go chronologically, from start to finish.

— *Description:* Provide specific details about what something looks, smells, tastes, sounds, or feels like. Organise spatially, in order of appearance, or by topic.

— *Process:* Explain how something works, step by step. Perhaps follow a sequence—first, second, third.

— *Classification:* Separate into groups or explain the various parts of a topic.

— *Illustration:* Give examples and explain how those examples prove your point.

Constructing Paragraphs

A paragraph represents a distinct logical step within the whole argument. That step may be big or little; it may take one or ten sentences to lay out—but the key is that it is one step. Thus there's no point in laying down as a rule (as one sometimes hears) that paragraphs should be four or five sentences long. That's probably a decent guideline for most paragraphs in student writing, but in good writing you'll find longer paragraphs and shorter paragraphs—some as short as a single sentence, if that's all it takes for that particular thought (use one-sentence paragraphs sparingly, but don't flinch from them when they're what you need).

Paragraphs are discrete steps in one's argument, but that doesn't mean that every step in the argument must fit within a single paragraph. Some complex thoughts may require so much space to explicate that the resulting paragraph would be two pages long. In such cases, break into smaller units, looking to subdivide along some sensible and clear scheme.

The basic idea is simple but crucial: When you write a paragraph, you should know what it is meant to do. If your answer is simply, "Well, this paragraph helps explain my topic," then you haven't thought deeply enough. How does this particular paragraph contribute to the argument? What logical step does it make? Where does it fit in the overall chain?

Readers like to know why they're reading a particular passage as soon as possible. That's why topic sentences placed at the beginnings of paragraphs are a good habit. A topic sentence, as its name implies, states the paragraph's topic—it need not state the paragraph's particular argument about that topic. That means that questions can make good topic sentences.

Here, fairly at random, are several good topic sentences, all placed at the beginnings of paragraphs:

— A popular audience for science, and for technology, blossomed in Europe and America in the 19th century. [*Examples follow.*]

— The third and final area of The ban expansion was by sea in the Aegean. Here again the enemy was Athens.... [*Detailed incidents follow.*]

— When we see a play, what is it that we see? [*An answer follows.*]

— A special sub case of realist theories deals with the balance of power. According to this version.... [*Elaboration follows.*]

There's no iron rule that topic sentences must come at the beginning of paragraphs, but if you keep in mind that you're writing to be understood, you'll tend to put them there. That's what readers are used to, and that's what they find easiest to follow.

Paragraphs should be constructed with some sense of internal order, whether through time, or space, or some other logical way or arranging information. Again, you have a lot flexibility in choosing an ordering scheme—as long as you choose something that will make sense to the reader.

It's common for writers to produce paragraphs that don't hang together, partly because we think as we write and don't always go back and revise thoughtfully. Here's an example, from an essay on Machiavelli's opinion about Christianity. This paragraph is really pasted together from two pieces (marked by italics):

> Christianity was not always weak and without vigour and war. When it was a new religion it extinguished the old, Paganism, in order to become the only one. In this, according to Machiavelli, Christianity behaved as every new religion does. The Christians burned the works of poets, threw down statues, and forbade Pagan teachings. *Their mistake in this overthrow was to keep the language of the Pagans, Latin. The Christians translated the Gospels into Latin, and Christian political leaders put wrote their civil codes in Latin. So, although they had blotted out all of the Pagan ceremonies and teachings, all was not forgotten. The works of great Pagan thinkers were still studied because the language was not extinguished along with the rest of Paganism.*

When the reader reaches the italicised portion, he gets a bit confused. The topic is the same, true—the early history of Christianity. But two distinct argumentative points are being made: (1) Christianity was once a fierce religion, and (2) Early Christians erred in not eradicating the Latin language. Each of these points deserves its own paragraph. The best test for deciding whether a paragraph hangs together is to read its topic sentence and see if it reasonably covers everything you discuss in the paragraph.

Linking Paragraphs

In a good essay, each paragraph should have some logical connection to the one before it. When your reader moves from one paragraph to the next, he knows that he has reached a new step in the argument. But that's all he knows. Is this new step another in the same direction, or is it a change? You have to guide your reader with appropriate signposts. One powerful type of signpost that many students think they can't use in essays is a direct question. When you want to move from one part of the argument to the next, it can be useful to start by asking a question that refers to what you just said but gives you room to move on: *What does this mean?* Or *Why does Plato think the noble lie is necessary?* Or *What evidence is there for this interpretation?* Good sharp questions can guide your reader through your argument.

Another way to link paragraphs is simply to write in such a way as to force the reader to recognise the link. Here's how one writer started a paragraph. Notice that it only makes sense in context, and that the writer was confident enough not to repeat material from the previous paragraph or make the link too explicit:

> The strange outcome was that the oil and energy crisis abated.

A less confident writer would have inserted a reference along these lines:

> The strange outcome of the several years of economic crisis afflicting Western and Arab states was that the oil and energy crisis abated.

When a writer lacks confidence in her essay's coherence, she'll be tempted to say things like this:

> Earlier it was mentioned that... As commented on earlier... As stated earlier... As stated before.. As I wrote before

These are awfully weak constructions. In the same camp is the word *also*, which is vastly overused as a connector at the beginnings of sentences, where it ıarely sounds very good:

> Also, Touchstone tries to get out of marrying Adore.

> Also, the data show that the reaction slows down as the temperature falls.

These nervous pointers (their sub-text is *Have I lost your attention yet? Have I confused you yet?*) Are poor substitutes for good organisation. Planning your argument and crafting coherent paragraphs that proceed step by step should make you feel able to dispense with such things. If on occasion you feel you have to use such a pointer, use a more conventional phrase like *as noted above*.

Process of Writing a Paragraph

While students often ask for advice on essay writing, few of them know that what decides about the ultimate quality of their papers is the ability to construct coherent paragraphs. Well-structured paragraphs help to both organise and present all thoughts and arguments that are supposed to be comprised in an essay. They also lead the reader toward the conclusion in a logical order.

In spite of the essay type in which they appear, all paragraphs should follow the same structural pattern. They begin with topic sentence which introduces main ideas of the whole paragraph. The following body paragraph contains arguments, examples, comparisons, etc. Terminator, the last sentence of a paragraph, serves as a conclusion to all the above. Alternatively, in longer essay forms terminator can be substituted by a transition sentence which marks the relation between following paragraphs.Many people need help writing a paragraph.

Getting Started on Your Paragraph

Before you start writing a paragraph, you need to decide two things. What are you writing about? What do you want to say? The purpose of any paragraph is to express an idea. Most paragraphs consist of a few related sentences. You can write a successful paragraph by starting off with a plan. The key to doing a successful paragraph is to break down the writing into short, simple steps.

Subject of your paragraph

Write down the subject of your paragraph. To express your subject, write only a word or phrase. Who or what are you writing about?

Pre-writing for your paragraph

Begin by brainstorming. Brainstorming doesn't involve writing complete sentences or paragraphs. Brainstorming involves coming up with ideas using words or short phrases. One popular way to create pre-writing ideas is to ask yourself questions about your subject. Here are some questions you might ask yourself:

— What do I know about this subject? How does this subject relate to me? What do I like or dislike about this subject? What words best describe it?

— Write only a word or phrase in response to each question.

Building the body of your paragraph

Reread all your words and phrases. Now, organise your thoughts. Decide if your brainstorming ideas are related. Do you want to add a new word or phrase or take something out? Next, decide if you like the order of your brainstorming ideas, or want to change the order.

Topic sentence

Topic sentence should be brief, clear and directly related to the paragraph content. It announces, yet in a neutral tone, what idea or problem is about to be discussed. It should give an idea of why a certain problem has to be considered in a given context. Moreover, topic sentences must not be referenced or quoted from secondary sources.

Reread the word or phrase about the subject of your paragraph. You are going to expand this into the first sentence of your paragraph. This first sentence, which comes at the beginning of a paragraph, is called the topic sentence. Remember that its job is to introduce your paragraph.

Paragraph body

Reread your brainstorming words or phrases for the body of your paragraph. Expand each brainstorming word or phrase into a complete sentence. These sentences explain your topic sentence by offering facts, details, or examples.

Remember that the job of your paragraph body is to share an idea with your reader.

The Body Paragraph consists of so-called detail sentences which describe and evaluate the problem mentioned in the introductory sentence.

Content of the Body Paragraph: it's composed of opinions, thoughts, arguments, quotations, etc. as well as obligatory commentaries on them. Unlike topic sentences or terminators, it can contain references, pictures, as well as contents in brackets.

Composition of the Body Paragraph:

— Visual elements such as charts, graphs and pictures as well as quotations and referenced paraphrases are never situated immediately after the topic sentence or right before the terminator. There must be at least one sentence introducing them and one sentence commenting on them.

— Organisation of sentences will vary according to essay type, but one rule holds for all – sentences should be of approximately the same length. They also shouldn't be too long or overlapped with very short sentences either.

— Paragraphs should be of more or less the same length to ensure clean structure. It is advised to avoid too short paragraphs; on average no more than three paragraphs can be situated on one standard formatted page.

— The weight of referenced material shouldn't outdo the author's own opinions and remarks.

Concluding Sentence

Reread your paragraph and then add another sentence that sums up the paragraph. This sentence ends your paragraph.

Closing sentences are not a summary of the paragraph but a restatement of its main ideas. In other words, terminator reflects on what was already presented in the body paragraph. Consequently, it will name conclusions rather than suddenly draw them. Transition sentences, in contrast to terminators, have the capacity to provide a short introduction to another paragraph explaining the order in which they were situated in an essay.

Revising the Paragraph

You've almost completed a paragraph. But you're not done yet. Every paragraph can be improved. The way to complete a successful paragraph is by looking over your work.

Try reading your paragraph draft aloud. Ask yourself questions. Do you like the order of the sentences in your paragraph? Do you need to add words so your sentences make better sense? Are there words you could put in to improve the connection between your sentences?

Do you like your introductory sentence? Your paragraph body? Your concluding sentence?

Make at least two changes that could improve your paragraph. Remember that even professional writers make lots of changes!

Proofreading

It's time to check your work. Read your improved paragraph aloud slowly. Look at details of punctuation and grammar in your writing. Are your sentences complete? Do your verbs go with your nouns? Do you need to add any missing punctuation? Have you used capital letters for names and addresses? How's your spelling? Remember that the job of proofreading is improves the way you express your ideas. Try catching and changing at least five mistakes.

7

Essay Writing

The word “essay” comes from the French *essai,* a try or attempt. The essay is an attempt to communicate information, opinion, or feeling, and usually it presents an argument about a topic. In the university context, an essay is an exercise that gives the student an opportunity to explore and clarify thoughts about a subject. In the larger world the essay appears in newspapers as opinion articles, editorials, reviews, and the more thorough commentary on news. If at times the essay form seems a little artificial, or removed from the kinds of writing you expect to produce when you leave university, remember that the skills you learn in thinking, organizing, researching, and writing will be required in almost any career. There will always be expository reports to write and arguments to present.

In recent times, essays have become a major part of a formal education. Secondary students are taught structured essay formats to improve their writing skills, and essays are often used by universities in selecting applicants. In both secondary and tertiary education, essays are used to judge the mastery and comprehension of material. Students are asked to explain, comment on, or assess a topic of study in the form of an essay. Academic essays are usually more formal than literary ones. They may still allow the presentation of the writer’s own views, but this is done in a logical and factual manner, with the use of the first person often discouraged.

Process of Writing Essay

In Greek legend, the goddess of wisdom, Athena, was born fully armed from the head of Zeus. Unfortunately, this is the only recorded instance of instant wisdom. Especially in the medium of the written word, the communication of complex ideas is a process—a process that requires thinking and rethinking, working and reworking. The student who claims to have dashed off an 'A' essay at one in the morning the night before it was due is either a liar or a genius.

Writing is a complex process; it is a learned craft which requires a lot of practice, and no formula can guarantee a good essay. What we suggest in the following section is a workable linear model for preparing and writing an essay—it could be summed up in a chart, thus:

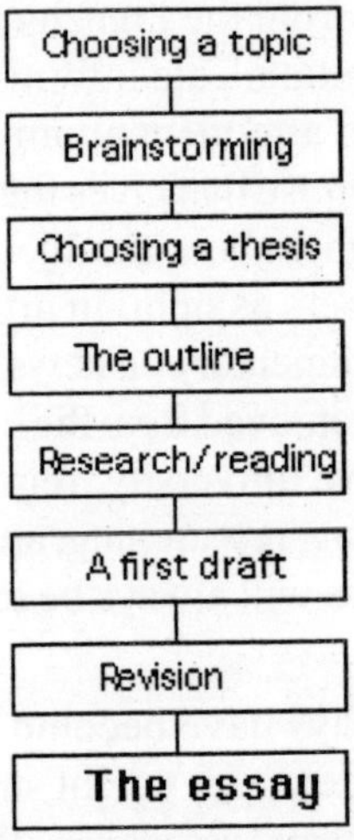

The important thing is to keep the simple model in mind. As you become more proficient, you will become more confident in developing your own study practices and writing techniques.

Getting Started

Narrowing Your Essay Topic

The first step in writing an essay is finding something to write about. Whether you are working from a list of assigned topics or selecting your own, try to find something which sparks your interest: not only will working on the assignment be more stimulating, but your commitment will also help you write a more convincing essay. Some preliminary reading may help determine how deep your interest goes, as well as letting you know what kind of material will be available as you write your essay.

A common problem of beginning writers is wallowing around in a topic too wide for their purposes. General words such as "media,""war," "life,"or "nature"are often incorrectly used as if they were topics (even "dragons"is too broad). However, students often begin to write essays with nothing more in mind than a general concept, and the result is a vague and generalized essay, of little interest to the student and less to the instructor. If you start with a broad area, concentrate on narrowing your subject,,it will also help you deal with your topic within the length of the paper assigned and the time you have been given to complete it.

You can narrow your topic by considering a particular approach to the subject, or a sub-topic within it. You might ask yourself key questions, such as the following:

Dragons

— Am I writing of one specific species of dragon, or of dragons in general?

— What kind of dragon do I wish to write about? Chinese? Fire-breathers? Kites?

— What activities, qualities, or myths of that particular dragon do I wish to explore?

War

— Am I writing of one war or of war in general?

— Which war do I wish to write about? WWI? WWII? The Gulf War? "War"taken more metaphorically,,between the sexes, siblings, or members of different races?

— Am I concentrating on the history of the war itself, or its causes or outcome?

— What specific events or examples will illustrate my points?

In deriving a workable topic from your subject, be careful not to narrow it too far; your topic must provide scope to develop a sustained presentation and argument.

— General subject: Media
— Narrowed topic: Commercials
— Specific topic: How commercials manipulate their audience
— General subject: Dragons
— Narrowed topic: Fire-breathing dragons
— Specific topic: Problems in fighting the medieval fire-breathing dragon.

The Thesis

All essays that involve the development of an argument require a thesis: the point you are arguing. While the topic is your subject, the thesis defines your position on that subject. Your essay will take a position and will provide convincing evidence to support that view. It is important to develop a working thesis early because it will help direct your thoughts and research; of course your thesis may change as your reading and writing progresses and you begin to incorporate new information.

Once you have chosen your topic, you can begin to formulate your thesis by thinking closely about it, doing some exploratory reading, or drawing from lectures or conversations with classmates and friends. One way to develop a thesis is to ask yourself questions about the topic and to focus on a central issue or problem which the topic raises. Your answer to this question will be your thesis.

Brainstorming

If you are having trouble developing a thesis, try brainstorming. You can brainstorm verbally with other people, or work alone, writing all your ideas on paper. The important thing about brainstorming is not to edit your thoughts. Write down everything which occurs to you about the topic, no matter how irrelevant or bizarre. The next stage is to make connections between your ideas, and to group them into sub-topics, expanding those that you can explore in more detail. Then see if you can put the groups into some kind of logical order, discarding those that do turn out to be irrelevant or bizarre. In most cases you will find that you have the beginning of an essay—something that implies a basic point of view you can explore further and refine into a fully developed argument.

There are several good books on using the brainstorming process to generate ideas for writing, including Tony Buzan's Use Both Sides of Your Brain and Gabrielle Lusser Rico's Writing the Natural Way. If you are still unsure about the topic, you should consult ycur instructor after you have done some thinking about the topic on your own.

The Statement of Your Thesis

Once you have discovered a thesis, sharpen it into a concise statement. The thesis statement usually appears in the introduction of your essay, and is best expressed in one sentence as a definition of your position, or the point you intend to prove in your essay. A good thesis statement will help organize your essay and give it direction; it is the central idea around which the rest of the essay is built.

The ideal thesis (like the topic itself) will be neither too broad nor too narrow for the compass of your essay. Clearly a 3000-word essay will have a more complex argument, and correspondingly a more complex thesis, than an essay of 600 words. One of the most common problems with essays is that they are based on a thesis that is too obvious to be worth arguing—a truism. Here are some examples of possible theses:

— *Specific topic:*

  How commercials manipulate their audience

— *A thesis that is a truism:*

  "Television Commercials attempt to sell their products to the largest possible audience."

— *A thesis that is too broad:*

  "Several tactics are used to entice consumers to buy the advertised product."(This thesis is likely to produce an essay that is simply a shopping list of examples, dull both for the writer and reader.)

— *A sharper thesis:*

"Commercials sell their products by suggesting that those who buy them will instantly enter an ideal world where they are irresistably attractive."

— *Too limited:*

"Molson Canadian commercials are offensive."

— *Specific topic:*

Problems in fighting the medieval fire-breathing dragon.

— *A thesis that is a truism:*

"Fighting fire-breathing dragons was hell."

— *A thesis that is too broad:*

"The flames of passion in courtly love claimed more knights' lives than all the fire-breathing dragons in medieval Europe." (The topic is unwieldy because it involves two areas of research, courtly love and fire-breathing dragons.)

— *A sharper thesis:*

"Fewer knights would have been broiled in their armour if the medieval world had known of fire-extinguishers."

— Too limited:

" 'Puff the Magic Dragon' is a sweet song."

It is possible, particularly when you are tackling an expository essay on a subject you know little about, that you will not be able to formulate a thesis, no matter how hard you storm your brains. In this case, the best strategy is to narrow the topic as best you can and to move straight to the process of writing an outline. Then you should begin your research and gather evidence .

Types of Essays

Five-paragraph Essay

Some students' first exposure to the genre is the five paragraph essay, a highly structured form requiring an introduction presenting the thesis statement; three body paragraphs, each of which presents an idea to support the thesis together with supporting evidence and quotations;

and a conclusion, which restates the thesis and summarises the supporting points. The use of this format is controversial. Proponents argue that it teaches students how to organise their thoughts clearly in writing; opponents characterise its structure as rigid and repetitive.

Academic Essays

Longer academic essays (often with a word limit of between 2,000 to 5,000 words) are often more discursive. They sometimes begin with a short summary analysis of what has previously been written on a topic, which is often called a literature review. Longer essays may also contain an introductory page in which words and phrases from the title are tightly defined. Most academic institutions will require that all substantial facts, quotations, and other supporting material used in an essay be referenced in a bibliography or works cited page at the end of the text. This scholarly convention allows others (whether teachers or fellow scholars) to understand the basis of the facts and quotations used to support the essay's argument, and thereby help to evaluate to what extent the argument is supported by evidence, and to evaluate the quality of that evidence. The academic essay tests the student's ability to present their thoughts in an organised way and tests their intellectual capabilities.

Descriptive Essays

Descriptive writing is characterised by sensory details, which appeal to the physical senses, and details that appeal to a reader's emotional, physical, or intellectual sensibilities characterise a description. Determining your purpose, considering your audience, creating a dominant impression, using descriptive language, and organising your description are the rhetorical choices to consider with a description. A description is usually arranged spatially but can be chronological or emphatic as well. The focus of a description is the scene. Description uses tools such as denotative language, connotative language, figurative language, metaphor, and simile to arrive at a dominant impression.

Narrative Essays

When creating a narrative an author must determine their purpose, consider their audience, establish a point of view, use dialogue, and organise the narrative. A narrative is usually arranged chronologically. The focus of a narrative is the plot. A narrative uses tools such as flashbacks, flash-forwards, and transitions that often build to a climax.

Exemplification Essays

A generalisation and relevant, representative, and believable examples including anecdotes characterise exemplification. A writer needs to consider their subject, determine their purpose, consider their audience, decide on specific examples, and arrange all the parts together when writing and exemplification essay.

Comparison and Contrast Essays

Compare and contrast is characterised by a basis for comparison, points of comparison, analogies, and either comparison by object (chunking) or by point (sequential). Comparison highlights the differences between two or more similar objects while contrasting highlights the differences between two or more objects. When writing a compare\contrast essay, a writer needs to determine their purpose, consider their audience, consider the basis and points of comparison, consider their thesis statement, arrange and develop the comparison, and reach a conclusion. Compare and contrast is arranged emphatically.

Cause and Effect Essays

The defining features of a cause and effect essay are causal chains, careful language, and chronological or emphatic order. A writer using this rhetorical method must consider the subject, determine the purpose, consider the audience, think critically about different causes or consequences, consider a thesis statement, arrange the parts, consider the language, and decide on a conclusion.

Classification and Division Essays

Classification is the categorisation of objects into a larger whole while division is the breaking of a larger whole into smaller parts.

Definition Essays

Definition essays are explanations of what is meant by a term.

Dialectic Essays

In this form of essay used commonly in Philosophy, one makes a thesis and argument, then objects to their own argument (with a counterargument), but then counters the counterargument with a final and novel argument. This form benefits from being more open-minded while countering a possible flaw that some may present.

Non-literary Essays

Visual Arts

In the visual arts, an essay is a preliminary drawing or sketch upon which a final painting or sculpture is based, made as a test of the work's composition (this meaning of the term, like several of those following, comes from the word *essay*'s meaning of "attempt" or "trial").

Music

In the realm of music, composer Samuel Barber wrote a set of "Essays for Orchestra," relying on the form and content of the music to guide the listener's ear, rather than any extra-musical plot or story.

Film

Film essays are cinematic forms of the essay, with the film consisting of the evolution of a theme or an idea rather than a plot per se; or the film literally being a cinematic accompaniment to a narrator reading an essay. From another perspective, an essay film could be defined as a documentary film visual basis combined with a form of commentary that contains elements of self-portrait (rather than autobiography), where the signature (rather than the life-story) of the filmmaker is apparent. The genre is not well-defined but might include works of early Soviet documentarians like Dziga Vertov, or present-day filmmakers like Michael Moore or Errol Morris. Jean-Luc Godard describes his recent work as "film-essays".

Choosing an Essay Topic

Topic Has Been Assigned

You may have no choice as to your topic. If this is the case, you still may not be ready to jump to the next step. Think about the type of paper you are expected to produce. Should it be a general overview, or a specific analysis of the topic? If it should be an overview, then you are probably ready to move to the next step. If it should be a specific analysis, make sure your topic is fairly specific. If it is too general, you must choose a narrower subtopic to discuss.

For example, the topic "KENYA" is a general one. If your objective is to write an overview, this topic is suitable. If your objective is to write a specific analysis, this topic is too general. You must narrow it to something like "Politics in Kenya" or "Kenya's Culture." Once you have determined that your topic will be suitable, you can move on.

Topic Has Not Been Assigned

If you have not been assigned a topic, then the whole world lies before you. Sometimes that seems to make the task of starting even more intimidating. Actually, this means that you are free to choose a topic of interest to you, which will often make your essay a stronger one.

Define Your Purpose

The first thing you must do is think about the purpose of the essay you must write. Is your purpose to persuade people to believe as you do, to explain to people how to complete a particular task, to educate people about some person, place, thing or idea, or something else entirely? Whatever topic you choose must fit that purpose.

Brainstorm Subjects of Interest

Once you have determined the purpose of your essay, write down some subjects that interest you. No matter what the purpose of your essay is, an endless number of topics will be suitable. If you have trouble thinking of subjects, start by looking around you. Is there anything in your surroundings that interests you? Think about your life. What occupies most of your time? That might make for a good topic. Don't evaluate the subjects yet; just write down anything that springs to mind.

Evaluate Each Potential Topic

If you can think of at least a few topics that would be appropriate, you must simply consider each one individually. Think about how you feel about that topic. If you must educate, be sure it is a subject about which you are particularly well-informed. If you must persuade, be sure it is a subject about which you are at least moderately passionate. Of course, the most important factor in choosing a topic is the number of ideas you have about that topic.

Even if none of the subjects you thought of seem particularly appealing, try just choosing one to work with. It may turn out to be a better topic than you at first thought. Before you are ready to move on in the essay-writing process, look one more time at the topic you have selected. Think about the type of paper you are expected to produce. Should it be a general overview, or a specific analysis of the topic? If it should be an overview, then you are probably ready to move to the next step.

If it should be a specific analysis, make sure your topic is fairly specific. If it is too general, you must choose a narrower subtopic to discuss. For example, the topic "KENYA" is a general one. If your objective is to write an overview, this topic is suitable. If your objective is to write a specific analysis, this topic is too general. You must narrow it to something like "Politics in Kenya" or "Kenya's Culture." Once you have determined that your topic will be suitable, you can move on.

Organise Your Essay

The purpose of an outline or diagram is to put your ideas about the topic on paper, in a moderately organised format. The structure you create here may still change before the essay is complete, so don't agonize over this. Decide whether you prefer the cut-and-dried structure of an outline or a more flowing structure. If you start one or the other and decide it isn't working for you, you can always switch later.

Diagram

1. Begin your diagram with a circle or a horizontal line or whatever shape you prefer in the middle of the page.

2. Inside the shape or on the line, write your topic.
3. From your center shape or line, draw three or four lines out into the page. Be sure to spread them out.
4. At the end of each of these lines, draw another circle or horizontal line or whatever you drew in the center of the page.
5. In each shape or on each line, write the main ideas that you have about your topic, or the main points that you want to make.
   — If you are trying to persuade, you want to write your best arguments.
   — If you are trying to explain a process, you want to write the steps that should be followed. You will probably need to group these into categories. If you have trouble grouping the steps into categories, try using Beginning, Middle, and End.
   — If you are trying to inform, you want to write the major categories into which your information can be divided.
6. From each of your main ideas, draw three or four lines out into the page.
7. At the end of each of these lines, draw another circle or horizontal line or whatever you drew in the center of the page.
8. In each shape or on each line, write the facts or information that support that main idea.

When you have finished, you have the basic structure for your essay and are ready to continue.

Outline

1. Begin your outline by writing your topic at the top of the page.
2. Next, write the Roman numerals I, II, and III, spread apart down the left side of the page.
3. Next to each Roman numeral, write the main ideas that you have about your topic, or the main points that you want to make.
   — If you are trying to persuade, you want to write your best arguments.
   — If you are trying to explain a process, you want to write the steps that should be followed. You will probably need to

group these into categories. If you have trouble grouping the steps into categories, try using Beginning, Middle, and End.

— If you are trying to inform, you want to write the major categories into which your information can be divided.

4. Under each Roman numeral, write A, B, and C down the left side of the page.
5. Next to each letter, write the facts or information that support that main idea.

Compose a Thesis Statement

Now that you have decided, at least tentatively, what information you plan to present in your essay, you are ready to write your thesis statement. The thesis statement tells the reader what the essay will be about, and what point you, the author, will be making. You know what the essay will be about. That was your topic. Now you must look at your outline or diagram and decide what point you will be making. What do the main ideas and supporting ideas that you listed say about your topic?

Your thesis statement will have two parts.

— The first part states the topic.
  — Kenya's Culture
  — Building a Model Train Set
  — Public Transportation
— The second part states the point of the essay.
  — has a rich and varied history
  — takes time and patience
  — can solve some of our city's most persistent and pressing problems

Once you have formulated a thesis statement that fits this pattern and with which you are comfortable, you are ready to continue.

Write the Body Paragraphs

In the body of the essay, all the preparation up to this point comes to fruition. The topic you have chosen must now be explained, described, or argued. Each main idea that you wrote down in your diagram or outline will become one of the body paragraphs. If you had three or four main ideas, you will have three or four body paragraphs.

Each body paragraph will have the same basic structure.

1. Start by writing down one of your main ideas, in sentence form. If your main idea is "reduces freeway congestion," you might say this: Public transportation reduces freeway congestion.
2. Next, write down each of your supporting points for that main idea, but leave four or five lines in between each point.
3. In the space under each point, write down some elaboration for that point. Elaboration can be further description or explanation or discussion.

   Supporting Point: Commuters appreciate the cost savings of taking public transportation rather than driving.

   Elaboration: Less driving time means less maintenance expense, such as oil changes. Of course, less driving time means savings on gasoline as well. In many cases, these savings amount to more than the cost of riding public transportation.
4. If you wish, include a summary sentence for each paragraph. This is not generally needed, however, and such sentences have a tendency to sound stilted, so be cautious about using them.

Once you have fleshed out each of your body paragraphs, one for each main point, you are ready to continue.

Write the Introduction and Conclusion

Your essay lacks only two paragraphs now: the introduction and the conclusion. These paragraphs will give the reader a point of entry to and a point of exit from your essay.

Introduction

The introduction should be designed to attract the reader's attention and give her an idea of the essay's focus.

1. Begin with an attention grabber. The attention grabber you use is up to you, but here are some ideas:

— *Startling information*: This information must be true and verifiable, and it doesn't need to be totally new to your readers. It could simply be a pertinent fact that explicitly illustrates the point you wish to make.

— *Anecdote*: An anecdote is a story that illustrates a point. Be sure your anecdote is short, to the point, and relevant to your topic. This can be a very effective opener for your essay, but use it carefully.

— *Dialogue*: An appropriate dialogue does not have to identify the speakers, but the reader must understand the point you are trying to convey. Use only two or three exchanges between speakers to make your point.

— *Summary Information*: A few sentences explaining your topic in general terms can lead the reader gently to your thesis. Each sentence should become gradually more specific, until you reach your thesis.

2. If the attention grabber was only a sentence or two, add one or two more sentences that will lead the reader from your opening to your thesis statement.
3. Finish the paragraph with your thesis statement.

Conclusion

The conclusion brings closure to the reader, summing up your points or providing a final perspective on your topic. All the conclusion needs is three or four strong sentences which do not need to follow any set formula. Simply review the main points or briefly describe your feelings about the topic. Even an anecdote can end your essay in a useful way.

Add the Finishing Touches

You have now completed all of the paragraphs of your essay. Before you can consider this a finished product, however, you must give some thought to the formatting of your paper.

Check the Order of Your Paragraphs

Look at your paragraphs. Which one is the strongest? You might want to start with the strongest paragraph, end with the second strongest, and put the weakest in the middle. Whatever order you decide on, be sure it makes sense.

Check the Instructions for the Assignment

When you prepare a final draft, you must be sure to follow all of the instructions you have been given.

— Are your margins correct?
— Have you titled it as directed?
— What other information (name, date, etc.) must you include?
— Did you double-space your lines?

Check Your Writing

Nothing can substitute for revision of your work. By reviewing what you have done, you can improve weak points that otherwise would be missed. Read and reread your paper.

— Does it make logical sense?

  Leave it for a few hours and then read it again. Does it still make logical sense?

— Do the sentences flow smoothly from one another?

  If not, try to add some words and phrases to help connect them. Transition words, such as "therefore" or "however," sometimes help.

— Have you run a spell checker or a grammar checker?

  These aids cannot catch every error, but they might catch errors that you have missed.

The essay must be well structured and presented in a way that the reader finds easy to follow and clear: it must look tidy and not present any obstacles to the reader. It must have a clear readable interesting style. But, above all, it must consist of your ideas about literary texts. This is the centre of it: this, and this only, gets the marks. Not quotes from critics, not generalisations at second hand about literary history, not filling and padding; your thoughts, that you have had while in the act of reading specific bits of literary texts, which can be adduced in the form of quotations to back up your arguments.

8

Letter Writing

Letter writing is a skill that students are likely to need at some point in their lives, regardless of where they end up—whether writing an absence excuse to their children's teacher, writing a letter of complaint to a store, writing a letter to the editor of the local newspaper, or writing a letter of appreciation or a thank you note to someone who has made a difference in their lives, all students, at one point or another, will end up writing a letter. Beyond the simple usefulness of the skill, letter writing makes a nice classroom assignment because it foregrounds issues of audience and the ways that audience affects tone, content, and style. Further, letter writing is a familiar kind of writing for most of our students — unlike literary analysis, letters are something our students are likely to sit down and write on their own, with nary a teacher in sight.

Better letter writing can result in proposals that win contracts, advertisements that sell products, instruction manuals that users can follow, billboards that catch a driver's attention. Stories that make us laugh or cry, and letters, memos, and reports that get your message across to the reader.

Organisation of Letters

Poor organisation is the number one problem in letter writing. As editor Jerry Bacchetti points out, "If the reader believes the content has some importance to him, he can plow through a report even if it is dull or has lengthy sentences and big words. But if it's poorly organised—forget it. There's no way to make sense of what is written."

Poor organisation stems from poor planning. While a computer programmer would never think of writing a complex program without first drawing a flow chart, he'd probably knock out a draft of a user's manual without making notes or an outline. In the same way, a builder who requires detailed blueprints before he lays the first brick will write a letter without really considering his message, audience, or purpose. Before you write, plan. As mentioned in the Pre-writing planning discussion earlier in this part, you should create a rough outline that spells out the contents and organisation of your letter, memo, report, or proposal.

By the time you finish writing, some things in the final document might be different from the outline. That's okay. The outline is a tool to aid in organisation, not a commandment etched in stone. If you want to change it as you go along—fine. The outline helps you divide letters and larger writing projects into many smaller, easy-to-handle pieces and parts. The organisation of these parts depends on the type of document you're writing.

There are standard formats for writing meeting minutes, travel reports, and many other business memos and letters.

If the format isn't strictly defined by the type of letter you are writing, select the organisational scheme that best fits the material. Some common formats include:

— *Order of location*. For example, a report recommending where to acquire new warehouses and parts depots based on the distance from the central manufacturing operation and the location relative to key accounts.

— *Order of increasing difficulty*. Instructions often start with the easiest material and, as the user masters basic principles, move on to more complex operations.

— *Alphabetical order*. A logical way to arrange a letter about vitamins (A, B, B1, and so on) or a directory of company employees.

— *Chronological order*. Presents the facts in the order in which they happened. Trip reports are sometimes written this way.

— *Problem/solution*. The problem/solution format begins with "Here's what the problem was" and ends with "Here's how we solved it."

— *Inverted pyramid.* The newspaper style of news reporting where the lead paragraph summarises the story and the following paragraphs present the facts in order of decreasing importance. You can use this format in journal articles, letters, memos, and reports.

— *Deductive order.* Start with a generalisation, and then support it with particulars. A lawyer might use this method in preparing to argue a case before a judge.

— *Inductive order.* Begin with specific instances, and then lead the reader to the idea or general principles the instances suggest. A minister might talk about different problems in the church caused by flaws in the building before asking for contributions to build a new roof.

— *List.* This section is a list because it describes, in list form, the ways to organise written material. A recent mailing from an electric company to its business customers contained a sheet titled "Seven Ways to Reduce Your Plant's Electric Bill."

Tone of the Letter

The best way to write your letters is in your own natural style. Having said that, there may be occasions during which you want to modify your natural style to better fit the occasion and your audience. For instance, if you are a naturally upbeat, cheery person, you would want to use a more sombre tone in a condolence note.

Let's look at four basic options for letter tone—forceful, passive, personal, and impersonal—including how and when to use each.

Forceful Tone

Forceful tone is used when addressing subordinates or others who, basically, have to do what you tell them to do. You are not asking them; you are ordering them in no uncertain terms—which you can do, because you have the power. This does not, however, give you license to be cavalier or crude. Indeed, the real skill is in getting people to follow your commands without harbouring ill will toward you. To achieve a forceful tone in your writing:

1. Use the active voice.
2. Be direct.
3. Take a stand.
4. Avoid hedge phrases and weasel words—language that equivocates rather than speaks plainly and directly (e.g., "might," "may," "perhaps").
5. Be clear.
6. Be positive.
7. Don't qualify or apologise.

Passive Tone

Passive tone is used when addressing superiors and others who, basically, you have to listen to and please—bosses, customers, clients. To achieve a passive tone in your writing:

1. Suggest and imply.
2. Do not insist or command.
3. Use the passive voice when possible.
4. Do not pinpoint cause and effect (e.g., solve the problem, but do not look to lay blame on the reader or anyone else).
5. Use qualifiers (for example, "might be," "may," "approximately," "roughly").
6. Divert attention from the problem to the solution.
7. Focus on the solution to the problem, rather than assigning blame.

Personal Tone

Personal tone is used when you want to give support or establish or improve a relationship. It is most appropriately used with people you know, rather than strangers, or at least with people whose situations you know about and empathise with. To achieve a personal tone in your writing:

1. Be warm.
2. Use the active voice.
3. Use personal pronouns ("I," "we," "you," and so forth).

4. Use the person's name.
5. Use contractions (we'll, it's, they're, can't).
6. Write in a natural, conversational style.
7. Write in the first person ("I") and in the second person ("you").
8. Vary sentence length.
9. Let your personality shine through in your writing.

Impersonal Tone

Impersonal tone is used when you either want to keep a relationship on a strictly professional level, or when you want to distance yourself from the other person or the subject at hand. Impersonal tone is also used when the relationship is adversary, or to stress the urgency and serious nature of the situation being written about. To achieve an impersonal tone in your writing:

1. Do not use the person's name.
2. Avoid personal pronouns when possible.
3. Use the passive voice when possible.
4. Write in the third person (for example, "the company," "the vendor," "the purchasing department," "the client").
5. Write in a corporate or formal style. 6. Be remote and aloof.

LENGTH OF THE LETTER

Whenever possible, keep your letter to one page. Today's busy readers really appreciate seeing that everything is on one side of a sheet of paper. Even Winston Churchill used to require of those serving under him that they express their concerns on no more than one side of a single sheet of paper.

If you have more to say, you can go to a second page, and possibly a third. No more than that. Exceptions include sales letters marketing products by mail (those can run four to eight pages or more) and family Christmas/holiday letters. For ordinary business correspondence, if your letter is taking up more than one side of two or three sheets, consider splitting the content between a shorter letter and an attachment or enclosure, such as a report. The art of being concise in your letter writing can require considerable effort in the rewriting and editing stage. Philosopher Blase Pascal once wrote to a friend and apologised for sending a long letter. He said, "I would have written a shorter letter, but I didn't have the time."

Layouts and Supplies

Do not overly concern yourself with questions of precise style. The reader does not really care whether the left margin is 1D 2-inch or 3D 4-inch, as long as the letter is easy to read. Here are a few quick rules for clear, easy-to-read letter layouts:

— Single-space copy; double-space between paragraphs.

— Indenting the first line of each paragraph five spaces makes the letter easier to read.

— Use generous margins—at least a half-inch bottom, top, and right, and maybe a little more on the left.

— Margins should be flush left and ragged right. Flush left means the first letters of each line are vertically aligned, creating a straight edge on the left. Ragged right means the right-hand border of the text is not neatly lined up.

— Do not try to cram too much text onto the page for the sake of keeping your letter to one page. It's better to either cut copy, or spread the copy out onto a second page.

— Sign in blue ink. It makes the live signature stand out more.

— Enclose your business card, unless you are sending a personal letter.

Type Styles, Fonts, and Sizes

Use a plain, simple type for body copy. Times Roman is clean and a favourite with many PC users. You can use New Courier or Prestige Elite, which gives the look and feel of a letter typed on an IBM Electric typewriter. Many older readers associate this look with a personal letter versus computer fonts, which look more impersonal.

Type size depends on the style selected. For New Courier, you can use 9- or 10-point type. For Times Roman, 11- or 12-point type is better.

Boldface and italic fonts can be used for emphasis. Bullets or numbers help set lists apart and make them easy to scan. For longer documents, you might consider breaking up the text into short sections, each with a boldface sub-head.

Letterhead

You can type your name, return address, and other contact information at the top of every letter on a plain sheet, or have letterhead made up by a printer. Many people have personal letterhead; virtually every business also uses pre-printed letterhead, adding the company name and logo at the top. Before you have your business letterhead printed, look at the layout prepared by your graphic artist or printer. Some layouts that take a creative approach may be graphically bold, but take up much space that could otherwise be used for letter text. Therefore you can fit far less copy on a single page than you would like, and are forced to use a second sheet (second page) to continue.

Much better is to have a letterhead design that allows maximum space for letter text. That way even if you have a lot to say, you can fit it comfortably on one page. "Second sheets" are pages of letterhead designed specifically to be used as the second and third pages in a multi-page letter. Some people use the same letterhead for every page, but this is unnecessary, unwieldy, and unusual. Most people use second sheets that have no printing on them, but are of the same paper stock of their letterhead. That way, the first and subsequent pages are all on the same stock.

Speaking of paper stock, your best bet is white, off-white, or cream coloured. These light colours allow major contrast between the paper and the black type. Letterhead that is gray, medium brown, red, or another dark colour makes it difficult for your reader to photocopy or fax your letter, which many people want to do.

Outer envelopes

The most common choice for business correspondence is the #10 envelope. A standard 81D2- by 11-inch piece of letterhead, folded twice horizontally into three sections, fits perfectly in a #10 envelope. If you have bulky enclosures, you may want to use a "jumbo," or 9- by

12-inch envelope. This allows you to enclose literature and other materials without having to fold them.

For personal mail, you can use either a #10 envelope or a smaller, Monarch envelope. The Monarch envelope has a slightly more personal touch, since businesses rarely use it. Monarch envelopes and stationery work well for short letters; for longer correspondence, standard #10 letterhead (fitting #10 envelopes) give more room for text.

On the back flap or in the upper left corner of the front of your envelope (known as the "corner card"), have your name and address for your personal letterhead. For your business letterhead, have your company name and address.

When you are sending correspondence or enclosed material that the customer requested, use a red rubber stamp with the words "Here is the information you requested" on the front of the envelope. This is an indication that the recipient asked you to send the letter and it is not unsolicited.

Stamps, Meters, Pre-printed Indicias

There are three ways to handle the postage for your letter: stamps, meters, and pre-printed indicias (pre-printed postal permits). The main thing when sending business letters is you want your letters to look like individual correspondence, not direct mail. The reason? Personal mail gets read, while promotional mail often gets tossed in the trash.

The postage stamp is the best choice for doing this. If you want to get extra attention, try using an unusual stamp, such as a commemorative. Another technique that gains attention is to use several stamps of smaller denominations instead of a single stamp for the correct amount.

Second-best to stamps is a postage meter. Enough businesses use postage meters for individual correspondence that it has an acceptable look and does not smack of advertising.

Least desirable is a pre-printed indicia. Since so many mass mailers use indicias in their direct mail campaigns, your reader might think your personal letter is direct mail (if you have used an indicia) and mistakenly toss it.

Even if your letter is direct mail and you are sending it bulk rate, a little-known fact is that you can use a third-class stamp instead of an indicia. This gives your direct mail a more personalised look, and hence a better chance of being opened and read.

Writing Personal Letters

If you read the personal !etters of literary and historical figures. You'll notice three things:

— The leisurely tone and pace of the letters

— The length of the letters

— The large volume of correspondence sent and received

As recently as the 1950s, writing personal letters was an important communications vehicle for intelligent, educated people. Even many "average folk", farmers, factory workers, day labourers, and homemakers—routinely wrote letters to friends and relatives.

People looked forward to letters: writing them, sending them, receiving them, and reading them. Getting letters was an unexpected, welcome event, like unwrapping packages on Christmas Day.

Today, personal letter writing is a declining art. The stories of our lives are now told in short, abrupt, unliterary, and un-grammatical e-mails instead of thoughtfully written letters penned in elegant handwriting. Yet people still write letters: brothers write sisters, college students write home to Mom and Dad, parents write loving letters to children who are spending their first summer at sleep-away camp.

Letters can still warm the heart, wash away fear and loneliness, and put a smile on Grandmother's face. The overriding instruction for personal letters: Write from the heart in a positive, caring, giving tone. Warm letters have always had a powerful ability to build goodwill. And in an age of computers and e-mail, the old-fashioned personal letter stands out even more.

Letters For Better Relationships

Some letters are written not merely to inform, but to strengthen the bond between you and the reader:

Letters of congratulations, thank-you letters, acknowledgments, "get well" letters, of condolence and sympathy, letters from the heart: All of these go beyond mere routine correspondence; if done well, they are written straight from the heart and create an emotional response (e.g., gratitude, pleasure, and warm feelings) in the reader.

In today's mass-communicated society, the greeting card industry has moved to relieve time-pressured consumers of the responsibility of writing relationship strengthening messages by writing generic messages in pre-printed greeting cards. As appreciated as greeting cards may be—sending one is a thoughtful gesture—personalise the message by inserting your own letter into the store-bought card. Another plus of writing letters by mail: Because most people write e-mail messages today rather than letters, sending a personal letter makes you stand out and has greater impact than other more expedient forms of communication.

Congratulation Letters

Achievement of a milestone—a birthday or anniversary, birth of a new child. Getting a new job, buying a home, winning an award, getting married, an anniversary—is an ideal reason to send someone a letter of congratulations. The reader will be pleased that you remembered the event and took the time to acknowledge it in writing.

Thank You Letters

In our fast-paced society, the polite act of writing thank-you letters has become increasingly rare. Many people prefer to thank people with a quick phone call or e-mail, rather than take the time to write and send a personal letter. A note of advice: Take the time. The extra effort will be appreciated and make you stand out from the crowd.If you don't write thank-you letters, start now. Thank-you letters are critical to maintaining good relationships. Conversely, not sending a thank-you letter when one is called for can harm a relationship. You may think that other people don't care if you send a thank-you letter—but they do.

A wide variety of occasions are appropriate for sending thank-you letters. The most obvious is when you have received a gift. You should also thank people for favours, friendship, and effort expended on your behalf.

Get Well Letters

Social custom dictates that you send a get-well letter to anyone close to you who has suffered a prolonged or serious illness. Is or has been hospitalised, or is recovering from an accident or surgery. If you send a get-well card, you can slip a letter inside it to add the more personal touch. In addition to the obvious benefit of bringing a smile to the face of a person who needs to smile more, your letter may actually help bring about their recovery. Numerous studies have identified a clear link between attitude and wiliness: Stress can make you sick, and positive emotions (faith, humour, happiness) can make you well.

Condolence Letters

A condolence letter expresses feelings of sympathy, care, empathy, and concern when a person close to the reader has recently passed away. Since there is nothing you can really say to make things right, say as little as possible. A few words from the heart and the fact that you took the time to send a personal note are the appropriate communication here.

Remember, you are writing not for the dead person, but for the loved ones he or she left behind.

- Share a personal story or pleasant memory about the deceased.
- Do not make any negative comment about the deceased.
- Do not minimise the reader's grief or sorrow, or the tragedy of the deceased's passing.

Sympathy Letters

Misery does not always love company, but when people have problems. They can get by a little better with some help—or at least a shoulder to lean on—from their friends.

A letter of sympathy is also a letter of empathy, helping other people get through difficult periods by showing that you understand and are there for them. Occasions that call for a sympathy letter can include personal injury or illness, separation or divorce, loss of a job or going out of business, failing a grade or dropping out of college, or any other unpleasant or negative occurrence.

Recommendation Letters

You will invariably be asked sometime in your life to write a letter of recommendation for someone seeking a job. If someone asks you in advance whether she can use you as a reference or have you write a referral letter, and you cannot in good conscience recommend her, say so. People who ask you to be references or write referral letters assume you will say positive things; after all, they are trying to get a job. Intending to write a less-than-glowing letter and not informing the person who asked you of your intention is like an ambush. If you cannot write a good letter of recommendation, decline.

There are two specific types of letters of recommendation. In the first type, a friend or colleague asks you to write a "generic" letter of recommendation. It is not for a specific job or employer, but meant to be a general reference she can show to interviewers if asked for such a letter. In the second type, the employer asks the candidate for references, and the candidate gives your name. The employer then asks you whether you recommend the person, and why.

If you have agreed to serve as a reference for a friend or acquaintance seeking a job, you may not want to write a separate letter for each position your friend is applying for. You can solve this problem by writing a blanket recommendation that the job seeker can show all potential employers.

Request Letters

A request is a letter asking the recipient to do something he or she does not have to do, may not have time to do, or may not want to do. Therefore, pay particular attention to the structure given for each letter; these are time-tested formulas for persuasive writing that have been proven to work. A letter is an ideal medium for requesting a favour. Making the request in writing allows the other person to think it over in the privacy of her own home or office, without the pressure of you standing there waiting for an answer, or the potential for embarrassment (for both of you) if you are turned down.

Complaint Letters

Unfortunately, there are many things to complain about in the world today. From poor service in a restaurant or store, to the high price of gasoline and rising income taxes. Complaints are often most effective when made in writing. There are two advantages to writing a complaint letter rather than talking about it. First, you feel better. And second, the person or organisation causing the problem takes you much more seriously when you commit your thoughts to paper.

Acceptance Letters

When you accept a job offer, confirm the offer and your acceptance in writing. Many companies do not use employment contracts, so if you are not given a contract, or the offer is not made in writing, your acceptance letter will document the terms and other particulars. This way, you have written proof of your position in case a dispute should arise.

If the offer is made verbally, take notes on what is said. Repeat back what you hear to make sure you have heard it correctly. Then sum it up in a letter to your new boss. Keep a copy for your files, and confirm both receipt of the letter and agreement to its terms and conditions.

Apology Letters

When you have had difficulty or a conflict with a person, a letter of apology can be effective in setting things right. Apologising by letter permits the other person to accept your apology, without argument or waffling. It also eliminates your desire to want to retract part of it or argue over the history of the incident.

At the same time, do not turn to letters simply to distance yourself from a difficult situation or protect yourself from a situation that may become confrontational. The advantage of letter writing is that you can take your time composing your thoughts, and the recipient can similarly take her time considering your message and deciding how to respond.

Agreement Letters

Letters of agreement are used to clarify working arrangements between two parties: a homeowner and a contractor; a consultant and a client; a vendor and a customer; a company department and senior management. When the relationship is customer/ vendor, a signed letter of agreement may serve as a contract between the parties.

Letters of agreement should accomplish several tasks:

— The letter must identify that it is an agreement to do work.

— The project should be named and described.

— It's also a good idea to thank the customer for choosing you or at least for allowing you to submit the agreement for consideration.

Other important items to include are cost, deadline, schedule, and payment terms. Be detailed and specific. If the agreement is unclear, vague, or ambiguous, it is the vendor, not the client, who is likely to suffer most, although it's generally bad for both parties.

Close by asking for the go-ahead—the return of the signed letter of agreement with any advance payment required.

Acknowledgment Letters

A specific category of thank-you is the acknowledgment of a gift given or a contribution made. An acknowledgment letter is similar to a thank-you note. If there is a difference, a thank-you note typically focuses on one short-term action, such as a birthday present you have received. An acknowledgment usually signifies something long term, such as the support a friend or relative has given you during a particularly difficult period.

Thank-you letters are event driven; for instance when your father co-signs for the loan on your first coned. An acknowledgment is emotion driven; for example, you feel an overwhelming need to thank your dad for all the love he has given you as a parent. Both thank-you letters and acknowledgments cement your bond with the reader. But an acknowledgment may be even more powerful because it is not expected. Acknowledgment is a spontaneous act, compared with thanks, which are expected as the social norm.

As its name implies, the letter of acknowledgment acknowledges a fact, situation, or action that has taken place, usually involving the recipient. According to Webster's New World College Dictionary, "acknowledge" means "to admit to be true, or as stated," but an acknowledgment letter does more than acknowledge; it also responds.

Often times, acknowledgements contain refusals or acceptances, or opinions and reactions. Your opinion and reaction may be mixed, with both positive and negative thoughts. Whenever stating a critique or opinion, give the positive first. Tell what you like and agree with. Then get to the negatives—what you don't like and what you want changed.

Regardless of whether your feelings are positive or negative, or whether you are accepting of or unreceptive to the situation or proposal before you, always start on a positive note and maintain a polite tone throughout your letter. In your acknowledgment, briefly recap the idea or proposal you are acknowledging. Do not repeat its history at length; the reader already knows it.

Sample Personal Letters

A letter of apology for rude behaviour

1234, Main Street
Boston, MA 02123

07 April, 2005

<Recipient Address Goes Here>

Hello,

I wanted to write to tell you how embarrassed and sorry I am for my behavior the other <day/night>. It was unforgivable of me to <description>, especially in front of my family. I wish I had a good excuse for what I did, but some things we just have to chalk up to stupidity and insensitivity. I really don't know what came over me.

I offer this apology from the deepest place in my heart and hope that you can bring yourself to forgive me for being so rude. I will do everything in my power to see that it never happens again.

Regards,

Jim Karter

encl: <List of enclosed items goes here>

A letter thanking gor a person for a gift

1234, Main Street
Boston, MA 02123

07 April, 2005

<Recipient Address Goes Here>

Hello,
I wanted to write to thank you for the wonderful <occasion> gift. I just love the <gift> you gave me. It's exactly what I wanted and I'm enjoying it immensely. You have a real knack for picking out the perfect present. It was so sweet of you to remember me with such a charming gift. Thanks again!

Regards,
Jim Karter

encl: <List of enclosed items goes here>

This letter gives a friend your support after a breakup.

1234, Main Street
Boston, MA 02123

07 April, 2005
<Recipient Address Goes Here>

Hello,
I am so sorry to hear that you and <name> broke up. I'm sure this is a time of adjustment and disappointment for you. It seems that no matter what a relationship was like, it always takes some time to get used to doing things without your "significant other."
I don't want you to feel that you're going through this alone. You have friends who care about you and want to be there for you. If you feel like getting out or just want someone to talk to, I hope you'll give me a call.
Please keep your chin up and let me know if there's anything I can do to make this time easier for you.

Regards,
Jim Karter

encl: <List of enclosed items goes here>

This letter just lets a friend know that you're glad to be so close.

1234, Main Street
Boston, MA 02123

07 April, 2005

<Recipient Address Goes Here>

Hello,

Sometimes it's easy to take our friends for granted. I was just thinking about how nice it is that we're friends and it occurred to me that I should tell you so! There have been so many times when I've thought, "Now what would I do without <name>?" You're always there for me and you always come through in a pinch. I always enjoy the time we spend together and usually wind up wishing we could get together more often.

I just wanted to let you know how glad I am that we're friends and how much our friendship means to me. Thanks for everything you do that makes you such a special friend.

Regards,
Jim Karter

encl: <List of enclosed items goes here>

WRITING BUSINESS LETTERS

Writing an effective business letter is an important skill for every manager and business owner. In this brief overview we will examine the five main steps in creating an effective business letter. With this knowledge you can quickly amend and personalise business letters.

Main Steps:

— Identify your aims
— Establish the facts
— Know the recipient of the letter
— Create sample Copy

— Decide on Physical layout of letter.

Identify your Aims:

Clearly establish what you want to achieve from the letter- whether it is to win back a dissatisfied customer or to reprimand an employee. Whatever the aim, create your letter from these goals.

Establish the facts:

Make sure you have the relevant accurate facts available. For a late payer, this might include relevant invoices, complaint forms, talks with your sales department and any previous correspondence from the customer.

Know the recipient of the letter:

Write in the language of your recipient. Try to put yourself in the position of the recipient. Read it from his point of view. Is the letter clear or open to misinterpretation.

If you know the recipient, use this knowledge to phrase the letter to generate your desired response.

Create a sample Copy:

Having established your aims, amassed the relevant facts with a conscious view of the recipient- write down the main points of your letter.

Decide on Physical layout of letter.

The physical appearance of a letter consists of the paper and the envelope.

The first thing a recipient sees is the envelope. It is essential that it is of suitable quality with the name and address spelt correctly. Quality envelopes and paper suggest a professional company.

It is wise to make sure the envelope matches the size of the paper. While you will use 81/2 x 11 inches (A4 size) sized paper for the majority of letters - a 4 x 6 inches (A5) can be used for specific shorter letters. But insist that correctly sized envelopes are used for this A5 size paper, allowing you maintain and convey an coordinated image.

Technical Layout

The following elements will constitute the formal outlay.

— Letterhead
— Name and address
— Date
— Reference
— Salutation
— Subject matter
— Communication
— Signature
— Enclosures

Letterhead:

This will include your company's name, address, telephone number, fax number and mail address. Include your web address if available. Other information may be required depending on the legal status of your business formation. Contact your legal adviser for exact details.

Name and address:

Always include the recipient's name, address and postal code. Add job title if appropriate. Double check that you have the correct spelling of the recipient 's name.

Date:

Always date your letters. Never abbreviate January to Jan. 31.

Reference:

These are optional. They are a good idea if you have a large volume of correspondence. These days modern word processors made this an easy task to complete and maintain.

Salutations:

The type of salutation depends on your relationship with the recipient.

Always try to personalise the letter thus avoiding the dear sir/madam situation.

Subject matter:

Again this is optional, but its inclusion can help the recipient in dealing successfully with the aims of your letter. Normally the subject sentence is preceded with the word Re: It should be placed one line below the greeting.

Communication:

This will contain a number of paragraphs, each paragraph dealing with one point and one point only.

Signature:

The signature should be clear and legible-showing you are interested in the letter and consequently the recipient. Your signature should also be followed underneath by a typed version of your name and your job title.

Enclosures:

If you include other material in the letter, put 'Enclosure', 'Enc.', or ' Encs ', as appropriate, two lines below the last entry.

Style of Business Letter

Previously we created the main points of our letter, now we must transform this into a final version. To do this, four main considerations are necessary.

— Format

— Prose

— Manner

— Accuracy

Format:

There are three main formats: blocked, semi-blocked and indented.

The former has all entries tight against the left -hand margin. The semi-blocked format sets the references and the date to the right margin for filing and retrieval purposes, with the remaining entries placed against the left margin.

The indented format follows the same layout as either of the above, but indents each paragraph by five or six spaces.

Prose:

Clarity of communication is the primary goal. Don't use technical jargon if the recipient is unlikely to understand it. Short sentences are less likely to be misunderstood or misinterpreted. Be precise, don't ramble. Check each sentence to see if it is relevant. Does it add to the point ?

Manner:

Always try to personalise your letters. Always try to be civil and friendly even if the subject matter is stern and sensitive. Give the impression to the recipient that some effort and thought has gone into the letter.

Accuracy:

Once the final version of the letter has been created, polish it off with a final spelling and punctuation check.

Types of Business Letters

Despite the widespread use of e-mail in commerce today, traditional business letters are still the main way that the majority of businesses officially communicate with their customers and other businesses. This is especially true when businesses want to formalise an agreement or an under-standing. So far, emails are great for all of the preparatory work, but a formal business letter is still most often needed to "seal the deal". There are two overall categories of business letters: business-to-business, and business-to-customer.

Business-to-business Letters

Most business-to-business letters are written to confirm things that have already been discussed among officials in meetings, on the telephone, or via e-mail. Can you imagine the letters that would have to go back and forth to cover all of the questions and possibilities that can be covered in a one-hour meeting, a half-hour phone call, or a few quick e-mails? The main purpose of a typical business letter is to formalise the details that were arrived at in those discussions, and to provide any additional information that was agreed upon. Over the years, certain general standards have evolved in the business world that the vast majority of businesses use in drafting their business to business correspondence. The top 10 business-to-business letters that people search are as follows:

— thank you letter
— introduction letter
— cover letter
— financial letter
— marketing letter
— sales letter
— project letter
— invitation letter
— employee letter
— congratulations letter

Even though the above terms are much more specific than the general term "business letter" there are multiple types of each of the above letters, depending on the purpose of the letter. For example, a business-to-business "financial letter" could be: collection letter, credit approval letter, credit refusal letter, invoice, price quotation, etc.

Business-to-Customer Letters

There are many different types of business-to-customer letters. They include: sales and marketing letters, information letters, order acknowledgement letters, order status letters, collection letters, among others. As with business-to-business letters, over the years certain general standards have evolved in the business world that the vast majority of businesses use in drafting letters to existing and potential customers.

Of course, going in the other direction are customer-to-business letters. These include: order letters, order status inquiry letters, complaint letters, and others. Since these are customer-generated letters, there is no particular expectation that they follow any particular letter- writing standard. Typically, they are handled just like any other piece of personal correspondence.

The top 10 business-to-customer letters are the following:

— cover letter
— customer relations letter
— financial letter
— credit letter
— introduction letter
— order-status letter
— sales letter
— marketing letter
— announcement letter
— apology letter

Similar to the situation with business-to-business letters covered in the previous section; even though the above business-to-customer letter types are much more specific than the general term "business letter", there are also multiple types of each of the above letters, depending on the purpose of the letter. For example, a business-to-customer "customer relations letter" could be any one of : response to a complaint, follow-up with a new customer, interrupted service notice, letter of acknowledgement, special invitation, welcome to new customers, etc.

Acknowledgement Letters

A letter of acknowledgement is good public relations maneuver. Though not always required, they can go along way. Remember, it's the thought that counts. The objective is to let the reader know you are in receipt of whatever it is was they sent; usually something requested in an inquiry letter. It can be viewed as a response to a response. The actual scope of an acknowledgement letter need only include a small detail, such as what day something arrived, and an expression of appreciation.

Adjustment Letters

An adjustment letter is a response to a written complaint. The objective is to inform a customer of a corrective measure that will resolve an unsatisfactory situation. It also serves as a legal document notifying the recipient that the complaint has been received and is being properly handled. Keep in mind that your reader has been inconvenienced and that this is a prime goodwill building opportunity. Everybody makes mistakes and owning up to one only adds to the customer's confidence in continuing a business relationship.

Complaint Letters

A complaint letter, also known as a claim, advises a business that an error has been made or that a defect has been discovered. The objective is to provide detailed information regarding the error or defect. It also serves as a legal document notifying the recipient that a correction or adjustment is being requested. Keep in mind that your reader is most likely a trained customer service professional and not the person responsible for the error or defect.

Rather than being angry, use a firm but courteous tone when stating your complaint. Remember, it is results you are after. The scope of a complaint letter should include only the relevant facts validating your claim and a request that appropriate corrective steps be taken. The scope may also detail the options that you are willing to accept in satisfaction of the claim.

Inquiry Letters

A letter of inquiry is a letter of request. The objective is to get the reader to respond with an action that satisfies the request. The action taken can benefit either the writer or the reader, and sometimes both. That being the case, the scope of an inquiry letter must include enough information to help the reader determine how best to respond.

Order Letters

An order letter, also known as a PO (purchase order) begins the paper trail of a specific purchase. The objective is to provide detailed instructions to a vendor fulfilling an order. It is also serves as a legal document recording the transaction. It should be written with careful attention to detail. Your intentions need to be clear and concise. The reader will fill your order only according to your instructions and your satisfaction will depend largely upon their accuracy. The scope of an order letter should include only the information needed to fulfill the order. Keep in mind that in most cases the seller does not need to know why you are placing the order, what it is going to be used for or for whom it is intended. Such information is unnecessary when placing an order.

Response Letters

A letter of response answers the questions asked in an inquiry letter. The objective is to satisfy the reader with an action that fulfills the request. Should you receive a letter of inquiry erroneously, or have neither the information requested nor the authority to reply, forward it on to the person in your company who does. Attach a memo to that person explaining your reason for forwarding the letter.If you are the correct person, be prompt with your reply. Address every question courteously, even those that seem errant or illogical. You must take into account that your reader probably lacks your expertise. Keep your response on point and on task, as short and complete as possible. Avoid going beyond the scope of the writer's request.

Elements of a Standard Business Letter

A good business letter is brief, straightforward, and polite. If possible, it should be limited to one single-spaced typewritten page. Because it is so brief, a business letter is often judged on small, but important, things: format, grammar, punctuation, openings and closings. A business letter is not the place to try out fancy fonts or experimental writing styles.

There are two main styles of business letters:

— *Full block style:* Align all elements on the left margin.

— *Modified block style:* Down the middle of the page, align the return address, date, closing, signature, and typed name; align other elements on the left page margin.

You will write business letters to inform readers of specific information. However, you might also write a business letter to persuade others to take action or to propose your ideas. Business letters even function as advertisements at times. Consider the letters long-distance phone companies send to those not signed up for their services or the cover letter to your resume. Both of these serve to promote or advertise. Business letters can be challenging to write, because you have to consider how to keep your readers' attention. This is particularly the case if your readers receive large amounts of mail and have little time to read.

Writing a business letter is like any other type of technical communication. First you have to analyse your audience and determine your purpose. The typical audience is other professionals. However, you might also write business letters to your co-workers. These audiences generally require you provide a detailed background about your purpose. Because a business letter is a communication from one person to another, a letter must convey a courteous, positive tone. Look at the situation from your reader's point of view and adjust the content and tone to meet the audience's needs.

Below are the elements of a standard business letter and their functions:

— the heading
— the date
— the inside address
— the salutation
— the body
— and the complimentary close
— an additional notation section often follows the close

Heading

— The heading is also the return address to which the recipient will refer when sending a response.
— The writer's name is not included in the heading, as it is appears in the complimentary close at the end of the letter. It should include only the street, city, state and zip code of the letter writer.

Identifying words such as Avenue, Circle, Court, Drive, and Street should be spelled out rather than abbreviated. Doing so reduces the chances of a response being sent to an incorrect address.

— The state name can be either spelled out or abbreviated in upper case letters according to U.S. Postal Service guidelines.

— The date a letter is written should be placed below the writer's return address information. It is the final component in the heading of a business letter.

The Inside Address

— The inside address contains the mailing information belonging to the recipient and should be justified to the left margin of the letter and placed two spaces below the date.

— As in the heading, the inside address includes the street, city, state and zip code of the recipient, all of which should be placed below the name of the business or organisation to whom the letter is being written. Identifying words such as Avenue, Circle, Court, Drive, and Street should be spelled out rather than abbreviated.

— When the recipient' name, title and position are known, they should be included as the first two lines in the inside address and placed directly above the name of the business or organisation.

The Salutation

— The salutation is a greeting. Its placement belongs two spaces below the inside address and always justified to the left margin of the letter. It should include the title and full name of the recipient, followed by a colon.

— Customarily the salutation begins with Dear, followed by a title such as Mr., Ms., Mrs., however, when the writer is on a first name basis with the recipient, that formality can be dropped in favour of a first name.

— The titles Mr., Ms., Mrs., and Dr. are always abbreviated. Other titles, such as Professor and Senator are never abbreviated. Regardless of marital status women should always be addressed as Ms.-the only exception being when the recipient has personally expressed a desire to be addressed otherwise (Miss or Mrs.).

— Avoid gender-based salutations when it is not known if the recipient is a man or a woman. Dear Student: Dear Customer: Dear Resident: etc. are perfectly acceptable options for gender-neutral correspondence.

— An impersonal device may be preferable when addressing a letter to a large organisation where the recipient's name is not likely to be known. For example, Attention: Accounts Receivable or Subject: Billing Error may replace more familiar forms of greeting.

— The salutation, To Whom It May Concern: is very out of date-very 20th Century.

The Body

— Begin the body of a business letter two spaces below the salutation or attention-getting device. Each paragraph should be single-spaced and justified to the left margin of the page with a double space separating each paragraph.

— It is acceptable to double space the text of a letter when the body is very short. This is done purely for cosmetic reasons, giving the letter a more visually balanced appearance on the page. In such instances it is appropriate to indent the first line of each paragraph.

The Complimentary Close

— The complimentary close is placed two spaces below the last line of a letter's body.

— Customary expressions used to close a formal business letter include Thank you, Sincerely, yours, and Yours truly. Less formal expressions such as Regards, Best regards, and Best wishes should be used only when the writer is addressing a business associate that is also a friend.

— When the expression contains two words, such as Thank you, only the first word receives an initial upper case letter

— A comma follows all forms of a complimentary close.

— Allow four spaces between the complimentary close and the typed version of the writer's full name. The space between is reserved for a handwritten signature. The writer's job position or title should appear directly below his or her name.

— The writer's signature should be identical to the printed version except in those situations where the recipient is also a friend, in which case a first name only is fine.

The Additional Notation

A number of situations call for a business letter to be marked with notations signifying those situations. These notations should be placed two spaces below the position or title line following the writer's printed signature.

When a letter references one or more documents that are enclosed by the writer for the recipient, the enclosure is noted in one of the following ways:

— Enclosure: Wholesale Pricing Packet

— Enclosures (5)

— Enc. (Encs.)

When a letter has been dictated to an assistant it should be initiated. Both writer and assistant are acknowledged with their personal initials. The writer's will appear in upper case letters and the assistant's will appear in lower-case letters in one of the following ways:

— EIB: pjc

— IMK/pjc

When copies of a letter are sent to named business associates or other interested parties, the copy recipients are acknowledged with their full name as.

Business Letter Formats

Business writers today generally favour the block or simplified letter formats for two reasons:

1. Moving all elements flush left is easier for typists/word processors.
2. Indenting is unnecessary, since one blank line is routinely left between paragraphs.

The modified block and semi block formats feel less formal than the block format. The choice of formats for business correspondence should be consistent with the image an organisation desires to project. Using the simplified format reduces the potential for the inadvertent use of sexist language, since the salutation is omitted. In the business world, the traditional greeting and closing are unnecessary.

Business letter formats include: basic-block style, modified block style semi-block style, simplified block style and full-block format.

— *Block:* Unintended paragraphs. All letter elements are flush with the left margin.
— *Modified block:* Unintended paragraphs. The return address, reference line, date, complimentary closing, and signature block are right of centre. Remaining elements are flush with the left margin.
— *Semi block*: Indented paragraphs. The return address, reference line, date, complimentary closing, and signature block are right of centre. Remaining elements are flush with the left margin.
— *Simplified:* The salutation and complimentary closing are omitted.
— *Full Block*: All elements of the letter are flush left.

Block Letter Format

The identifying feature of the *block* style letter is the left justification of all structural parts of the letter except for the following:

— the dateline
— the complimentary close
— the signature line.

The dateline is placed to the right of centre, and may be moved to coordinate with the letterhead. The complimentary close and the signature line are typed to the right of the horizontal centre of the page.

Use the exercise that follows to explore block letter style formatting. With the block letter style each paragraph begins on the left margin. Some more important information continues in the first paragraph for two to four sentences.

Between paragraphs there is additional line space indicating a new paragraph. As before, this paragraph begins at the left margin, as do, receiver's address, salutation, and additional information. However, the date of composition, complimentary close, sender's name, and title are placed right of centre. This makes the block style both functional and a bit more stylised in composition.

Sample of block letter

121 Knox Road #6
Denver, Colorado 80122
March 4, 20—
Linda Hennessee
Managing Editor
World Discovery
1650 K. Street, NW
Washington, DC 20036

Dear Ms. Hennessee:

I am applying for the summer editorial internship you listed with the career Development Centre at the University of Maryland. I am currently a junior at the University of Denver, with a double major in English and Latin American Studies.

Over the past three years I have gained considerable experience in newspapers and magazine journalism.

I am available for an interview almost any time and can be reached at 303-740-3148. I will be in Virginia from April 4 to April 12; if you want to contact me there, the number is 703-555-2006.

I look forward to hearing from you.

Sincerely

Jeffrey Richardson

Modified Block Letter Format

Another style to use for business letters is the modified block style. Several lines begin near the middle of the page:

— The return address

— The date

— The closing

— The handwritten signature

— The typed name

All the other parts begin at the left margin. Each paragraph of the body is indented.

Sample of modified block letter

65 Springtooth Road
Atwater, CA 95301
August 20, 2002
Mrs. Bernard
Summer Clothes Inc.
16 Cassy Drive
Burbank, CA 65656-6565
Dear Mrs. Bernard:

This letter is in response to your advertisement in the Modesto Bee. I would like to apply for the position of sales agent for Summer Clothes Inc. I understand that this position is temporary and will last only during the summer season.

For the past year, I have been employed at a clothing store. My duties included customer service, selling clothing, and using a cash register. I believe I have the experience nesessary to be a sale agent.

I will call you on March 2. You may reach me at 209-000-0000 before then. I am available any time for an interview.

Thank you for considering me for this position.

Sincerely,
Julie Coate

Semi-block Letter

The semi-block letter is a more traditional letter format than the full-block or block.

The identifying features of the semi-block style letter is the left justification of the inside address and salutation and the indentation (five to ten spaces) of the first line of each paragraph. The dateline is placed to the right or to harmonise with the letterhead. The complimentary close and the signature line are typed to the right of the horizontal centre of the page.

With the semi- blocked letter style each paragraph begins with a five to ten space indent. Some more important information continues in the first paragraph for two to four sentences.

Between paragraphs there is additional line space indicating a new paragraph. As before, the paragraph has a first line indent. The date of composition, receiver's address, complimentary close, sender's name, and sender's title are set right of centre. The additional information is left aligned.

Sample of semi-block letter

121 Knox Road #6
Denver, Colorado 80122
March 4, 20—
Linda Hennessee
Managing Editor
World Discovery
1650 K. Street, NW
Washington, DC 20036

Dear Ms. Hennessee:

I am applying for the summer editorial internship you listed with the career Development Centre at the University of Maryland. I am currently a junior at the University of Denver, with a double major in English and Latin American Studies.

Over the past three years I have gained considerable experience in newspapers and magazine journalism.

I am available for an interview almost any time and can be reached at 303-740-3148. I will be in Virginia from April 4 to April 12; if you want to contact me there, the number is 703-555-2006.

I look forward to hearing from you.

Sincerely,

Jeffrey Richardson

Simplified Letter Style

Some professionals believe that neither the salutation nor the complimentary close are read, and therefore neither should be included. This has produced the "simplified letter style." A very good use of the simplified letter style is when you cannot identify the name or gender of the person to whom you are writing. Instead of using a generic "Dear Sir or Madam" salutation, skip the salutation entirely and just identify the subject.

Sample of simplified letter

121 Knox Road #6
Denver, Colorado 80122

March 4, 20—-

Linda Hennessee
Managing Editor
World Discovery
1650 K. Street, NW
Washington, DC 20036

I am applying for the summer editorial internship you listed with the career Development Centre at the University of Maryland. I am currently a junior at the University of Denver, with a double major in English and Latin American Studies.

Over the past three years I have gained considerable experience in newspapers and magazine journalism.

I am available for an interview almost any time and can be reached at 303-740-3148. I will be in Virginia from April 4 to April 12; if you want to contact me there, the number is 703-555-2006.

Sincerely

Jeffrey Richardson

Full-Block Format

The identifying feature of a full-block letter style is the left justification of all ten structural parts of the letter. You may review the parts by going from list to the illustrated letter, using the numbers as the identification link. You may review the names by working from the letter to their identification in the list. The name in itself is not that important, but they help as a reminder to be aware of their consistent placement in letter composition. With the full-block letter style each paragraph begins on the left margin. Some more important information continues in the first paragraph for two to four sentences. Between paragraphs there is additional line space indicating a new paragraph. As before, this paragraph begins at the left margin, as do the date of composition, receiver's address, complimentary close, sender's name, title, and additional information.

Sample of full-block letter

121 Knox Road #6
Denver, Colorado 80122
March 4, 20—

Linda Hennessee
Managing Editor
World Discovery
1650 K. Street, NW
Washington, DC 20036

Dear Ms. Hennessee:

I am applying for the summer editorial internship you listed with the career Development Centre at the University of Maryland. I am currently a junior at the University of Denver, with a double major in English and Latin American Studies.

Over the past three years I have gained considerable experience in newspapers and magazine journalism.

I am available for an interview almost any time and can be reached at 303-740-3148. I will be in Virginia from April 4 to April 12; if you want to contact me there, the number is 703-555-2006.

I look forward to hearing from you.

Sincerely,

Jeffrey Richardson

WRITING COVER LETTERS

Writing cover letter and resume is like an art. You need to understand clearly what should go it in and what should not.

Cover Letters

Cover letter is a letter which is sent with a proposal to provide some additional information and highlighting your interest in the job. Your should write a resume cover letter which shows your unique background fitting the needs of the company and compels the recruiter to call your for an interview. Make your cover letter aligning with your job profile and the needs of the job. Cover letters are important because they underline not only your resume, but also your writing style, personality, and attitude, as well as your attention to detail. A cover letter is used to:

— Introduce yourself and ask for consideration of your qualifications for a position with that organisation.

— Summarise your qualifications for a particular position or for any position in that organisation.

— Direct the employer's attention to something specific on your enclosed resume concerning your background and their needs.

— Communicate your interest in and enthusiasm for the position and that employer.

— Ask the employer for an interview.

A cover letter introduces you and your resume to an employer, and you should send a cover letter with every resume you submit. In your cover letter, state why you are writing, why you are the best person for the job, and when you plan to contact your prospective employer. Many people think that a cover letter is not as important as a resume.

Actually, a cover letter is very important, because it gives you the opportunity to draw your readers' attention to specific qualifications. A resume presents a lot of information about your past employment and education, while a cover letter features specific qualifications that you think will impress your readers the most.

A cover letter is also important because it provides a sample of your written communications skills. Showing you can write well will demonstrate your intelligence and help to establish your credibility.

Always write cover letters with care, because, like resumes, cover letters create an image of who you are as a professional. You should plan to write a new cover letter for every position you apply for, because cover letters should be tailored to the needs of your readers. An employer seeking an electrical engineer, for instance, will be impressed by a different letter than an employer seeking a mechanic. Always bear in mind that the content of your cover letter should change from job to job.

Your application letter is one of your most important job-search documents. An effective letter can get you a phone call for an interview, but a poorly written application letter usually spells continued unemployment. The difference can be a matter of how you handle a few key points.

In many job applications, you attach an application letter to your resume. Actually, the letter comes *before* the resume. The role of the application letter is to draw a clear connection between the job you are seeking and your qualifications listed in the resume. To put it another way, the letter matches the requirements of the job with your qualifications, emphasising how you are right for that job. The application letter is not a lengthy summary of the resume—not at all. It selectively mentions information in the resume, as appropriate.

Types of Cover Letters

To begin planning your letter, decide which type of application letter you need. This decision is in part based on requirements that employers may have, and in part based on what your background and employment needs are. In many ways, types of application letters are like the types of resumes. The types of application letters can be defined according to amount and kind of information:

— *Objective letters*—One type of letter says very little: it identifies the position being sought, indicates an interest in having an interview, and calls attention to the fact that the resume is attached. It also mentions any other special matters that are not included on the resume, such as dates and times when you are available to come in for an interview. This letter does no salesmanship and is very brief.

— *Highlight letters*—Another type of application letter, the type you do for most technical writing courses, tries to summarise the key information from the resume, the key information that will emphasise that you are a good candidate for the job. In other words, it selects the best information from the resume and summarises it in the letter—this type of letter is especially designed to make the connection with the specific job.

Writing of Effective Cover Letters

Cover letters should be tailored to the needs of specific employers. For this reason, you should aim to include information in your cover letter that is related to the position for which you are applying. This information should persuade your readers you are the best person for the job. Before writing your letter, it is important to know that employers desire different kinds of people for different positions. For instance, an employer seeking an accountant may desire someone with bookkeeping abilities and an accounting degree, while an employer seeking a human relations coordinator may desire someone who works with other people and has proven leadership skills. Applicants for these jobs should highlight in their cover letters qualifications related to these positions.

Further, different employers hiring for the same type of position may not desire the same kind of applicant. For instance, two companies may advertise a position in public relations. One company may desire someone with a public relations degree and strong communications skills, while the other company may desire someone with the ability to work with people from different cultures. A person applying for the first company should include information about his or her degree and communications skills, while a person applying for the second company should include proof that he or she can work with all kinds of people

The cover letter is every bit as important as your resume. In fact, many employers will not even look at your resume if the cover letter is poorly written, disorganised or difficult to read and understand. And of course, if your resume isn't even read, the chance of getting an interview is virtually zero. Therefore, it is important to give the same careful consideration and attention to the preparation of cover letters as you gave to your resume. There are basically two types of cover letters you might use in your job search:

— *Letter of Application or Response to an Advertisement*: used when you are responding to a specific advertised opening; the strategy here is to show how your skills and qualifications fit the requirements of the position.

— *Letter of Inquiry*: used when you are contacting an individual or organisation to ask about possible openings; the strategy is the same except that you focus on broader occupational or organisational requirements to demonstrate how your qualifications match the work environment or can be utilised to meet organisational needs.

Whichever type of cover letter you are sending, it says something very important about you as a professional and as a prospective employee. It should be a clear demonstration of your written communication skills and knowledge of accepted business practices, as well as your ability to convince and persuade the reader of your value to the organisation. This means that you must *prepare a new letter each time—after doing some research* to determine the particular needs and requirements of the organisation and position you are seeking. You must also determine which of your specific skills or accomplishments best demonstrate how you can meet those needs. Finally, you must compose a letter that communicates your value in an understandable, concise, professional and businesslike way.

The opening salutation should be the name of whomever you are writing to. You should try to find out who will be reading your letter. If you cannot, write Human Resources Director, or the appropriate title. Never write "Sir," or "Madam," or any combination of the two, because it sounds too formal, and you may make a mistake about the person's gender. Another mistake is to write "to whom it may concern," since this is too nonspecific. Follow the salutation with a colon as opposed to a comma.

The first paragraph should state your reasons for writing, identify the position that you are interested in, and why you are interested in joining the organisation. If someone has referred you, mention it here to make the impression that you are an insider. This paragraph should be no longer than 2-3 sentences.

For the second paragraph, highlight your educational credentials, employment experiences, and the attributes that qualify you for the job. Use specific examples if possible to demonstrate your leadership abilities, communication skills, et. This paragraph should be no longer than 3-4 sentences.

Elements of a Cover Letter

Your Name
Your Address
City, State Zipcode
Your Phone Number

Date of Letter

Reader's Name
Reader's Title
Name of Company
Company Address

Salutation: Use Title and Last Name if available; don't use a first name unless you know the individual well and are sure this is acceptable; if you do not have a name, use the title. If you have the name but aren't sure whether the individual is a male or female, use the full name with no title (e.g., Dear Terry Johne's).

Opening Paragraph: State why you are writing, name the position or type of work for which you are applying and mention how you heard of the opening or organisation.

Middle Paragraph(s): Here you want to describe your major strengths as they relate to the position you are seeking. If possible, mention one or two recent accomplishments that illustrate your proficiency and effectiveness. The idea is to create interest and show how your skills and qualifications can be of value to the organisation.—To make the reader want to know more. Don't reiterate everything that's in your resume, but refer the reader to your enclosed resume for more detail on your qualifications and experience.

Closing Paragraph: Restate your strong interest in the position or organisation and your desire for a face-to-face meeting. Pave the way for the interview by indicating the action or steps you will take to initiate a meeting. If this is not appropriate, simply state that you look forward to hearing from the reader soon. Finally, express your appreciation for the reader's time and consideration.

Sincerely,

Your full name
Enclosure

Organising the Cover Letter

A cover letter has four essential parts: heading, introduction, argument, and closing.

- A heading provides your contact information, the date you're writing, and the address of the company to which you are applying.
- An introduction begins with a greeting, such as "Dear Ms. Dawson," followed by a statement of who you are and why you're writing.
- In your argument, you should describe the most important qualifications that prove why you are the best person for the job.
- A closing reveals what you plan to do after your readers have received your resume and cover letter. Your letter ends with a salutation and signature, such as "Sincerely," or "Sincerely Yours."

Heading

In your heading, include your contact information, such as your name, address, phone number, fax number, and e-mail address. Do not forget to include your e-mail address and phone number, because employers will often call you at home or contact you via e-mail.

After you have included your contact information, skip a space, and then write the date, such as "September 12, 2002." Skip another space, and write the contact information of the company to which you are applying. If you are writing to a specific person, be sure to include both his/her name and title, if the title is available. For example, "Catherine Lennox, Vice President of Public Relations." Follow this line with the address of the company.

For example:

Gina E. Pastoli
503 Bridge St.
Homewood, IL 60430
708-555-0293
gpastoii@e-mail-link.com

September 12, 2002

Catherine Lennox, Vice President of Public Relations
Taylor, Krammer, & Smith Associates
43 Westminster Ave.
Madawaska, ME 04756

Addressing the Letter

Whenever possible, you should address your letter to a specific individual, the person in charge of interviewing and hiring (the hiring authority). The reason for this is that larger companies often have standard procedures for dealing with solicited and unsolicited resumes and cover letters. To avoid having your materials filed away, it would be best to send them directly to a hiring authority.

When a job advertisement does not provide you with the name of the hiring authority, call the company to ask for more information. Even if your contact cannot tell you the name of the hiring authority, you can use this time to find out more about the company.

If you cannot find out the name of the hiring authority, you may address your letter to "hiring professionals" - e.g., "Dear Hiring Professionals."

Writing the Introduction

Begin your introduction with a greeting, such as "Dear Mr. Roberts." If your contact has a name like "Randie Owns" or "Pat Jenkins," and you are uncertain of his/her gender, address the letter "Dear Randie Owns."

In your introduction, begin by stating who you are and why you're writing. For example, if you're a student, state what university you're attending, what your major is, followed by the position you seek.

When you know your reader or have a connection to your reader, use your introduction to personalise your cover letter. You may mention the name of a professor who suggested you apply to the company, or a family member who works there. For example, "Professor Smith speaks highly of Turner Construction, and he advised me to write directly to you." If you drop any names, however, be sure that your reader has a positive relationship with the person you mention.

You can also bring up any previous conversations or meetings you've had with your reader. If you met your reader only once at a career fair, for instance, refer to a specific topic of conversation to remind him or her who you are, and then show your reader that you've been thinking about the conversation. For instance, "I've been thinking about our conversation at Pursue's Career Fair on Monday, February 12. I agree that a friendly disposition and strong work ethic are essential to success, and I believe I can bring these attributes to your corporation."

Writing your Argument

Your argument is the most important part of your cover letter, because it allows you to persuade your reader why you are the best person for the job. Carefully choose what to include in your argument, because you don't have much space. You want your argument to be as powerful as possible, but you don't want to bog down your reader in excessive details about your past.

In your argument, you should aim to:

— Show your reader you possess the most important skills s/he seeks.

— Convince your reader that the company will benefit from hiring you.

— Write two to three short, well-written paragraphs.

— Include in each paragraph a strong reason why your employer should hire you.

— Avoid explaining your resume.

— Maintain a friendly tone.

When writing your argument, remember that it is essential for you to learn as much as possible about the best person for the job. What kind of individual is your potential employer most likely to hire? What kind of skills, work experience, and degrees would this person have? Once you have answered these questions, ask yourself how you can show in your argument that you are the person your prospective employer seeks.

To learn about the best person for the job, you should read your job advertisement carefully, learn what a company values, and talk to people with "inside information." Through completing these steps, you should learn what qualifications are most important for a specific position.

When writing your argument, try to answer the following three questions:

1. Why am I qualified for this position?
2. How can I prove I'm qualified for this position?
3. What have I done that sets me apart from other candidates?

Writing about Your Qualifications

Once you know what the most important qualifications are for a position, you should show your reader you possess these qualifications. This will help you to accomplish your primary goal: to convince your reader you are the best person for the job.

When proving you're qualified for a position, we recommend highlighting your transferable skills. A transferable skill is an ability you utilised in your past that can be used at your next place of employment. For example, if you learned to use specific technical applications through a previous job, and a potential employer seeks a candidate who can use these applications, your ability to use them is a transferable skill.

Transferable skills are worth featuring in your cover letter because they demonstrate why you are right for the position. They show you can meet your reader's expectations, because you have used the skills he or she seeks at a previous place of employment.

Before deciding which transferable skills to include in your argument, make sure that the skills you wish to feature are important to the position for which you are applying. For instance, if you used interpersonal skills at a previous place of employment, but these skills are not essential to the position you seek, we suggest highlighting other skills your reader would be more interested in.

Let's look closely at Debark Johne's, an individual applying for a position in human resources. The most important qualifications for this position are three years of experience in the field, the ability to work independently, and written communication skills. We recommend that

Ms. Johne's prove to her reader she possesses these qualifications. Perhaps she would write the following in her argument:

> I worked for the city of Leafage's department of human resources for four years. My supervisor (Jacob Seamier) often gave me independent projects without deadlines, so I set my own schedule. I always finished my projects within two weeks of receiving them, demonstrating my ability to work independently. Mr. Seamier also made me his 'personal editor,' as he gave me copies of reports to edit for content, grammar, and punctuation. Combined with my experience writing memos and letters, this experience shows strong written communication skills.

Think of your argument as a series of statements about your abilities, followed by proof that your claims are true. For example, if you claim to have expertise in a specific field, show how you gained this expertise. Did you gain it through obtaining a degree, working in your field, or both?

It is common for cover letter writers to make claims about their abilities without proving their claims are true. For instance, a job applicant may write, "I have strong interpersonal and written communications skills." If the author does not go on to discuss these qualifications in more detail, a reader will not know whether these claims are true.

To persuade a reader that the author has these skills, she might want to write the following:

> I have strong interpersonal skills, which I gained from working as a server at Tom's American Restaurant while going to school. At Tom's, I learned to work well with other employees, while putting the needs of customers first. I also have experience with writing in the workplace. When I was an intern at New berry & Johne's, I wrote memos and letters to customers and colleagues on a daily basis. This experience taught me to write professionally and to-the-point.

Note that the author of this paragraph uses transferable skills to demonstrate her interpersonal and written communication skills. She focuses on her experience working with colleagues and customers at a previous place of employment, and then she features her familiarity with writing day-to-day business correspondence.

To capture your potential employer's interest, it is important to know what sets you apart from other candidates. Before writing your argument, it is important to think carefully about everything you've done that makes you impressive. Try to focus on accomplishments, awards, and special projects.

Accomplishments

An accomplishment is something you've done that most other individuals with your level of experience have not. Accomplishments can be professional, academic, or personal. The best kind of achievement to mention in your cover letter is a professional accomplishment. These accomplishments are impressive to potential employers because they demonstrate you can make decisions that will improve their business. A professional accomplishment is something you did at a former place of employment that helped to improve your employer's efficiency and productivity.

If you claim to have improved a former employer's productivity, however, be sure to show how you achieved this goal, and explain the outcome in precise numbers. For instance, if you instituted a program that improved the rate of employee retention, describe the program, and give the figures that prove the retention rate improved.

Another kind of professional accomplishment involves working part- or full-time while going to school. Employers are enthusiastic about college graduates who financed their own education, because this experience demonstrates an ability to work hard, to set and achieve goals, and to handle multiple tasks. If you paid for your own education, consider mentioning this in your cover letter.

If you are a student who does not yet have professional accomplishments, focus on academic and personal accomplishments. An academic accomplishment is something you did in school that shows you have skills your employer seeks. For example, you may have attained a high GPA while participating in multiple activities, demonstrating your ability to complete multiple tasks with excellence. Or you may have organised a formal event for your sorority or fraternity, demonstrating leadership skills. Try to focus on anything you did in school that your potential employer would be interested in.

Another kind of achievement you can feature is a personal accomplishment, something you did that you're proud of. It can be a goal you set and accomplished, or a passion you have for your work. For example, you may have played on your basketball team in college, and you set out to give your best efforts to the team. You may want to mention in your argument that your commitment to playing well improved the team's success. Or, perhaps you dreamed of working in the fashion industry since you were a child, and you were able to realise this dream through studying fashion. Featuring these items in your cover letter will help to give your reader confidence that you have a desire to carry out goals, and that you are capable of outshining others.

Awards

Awards are important to feature in cover letters because they show that others have recognised the high quality of your work. If you mention an award in your cover letter, however, do not assume that your reader knows anything about the award or the context in which you won it. Be sure to say something about the competition and the number of competitors. The best kind of award to feature in a cover letter is one related to the position you seek. For instance, a candidate applying to law school may want to mention that she was selected by her undergraduate professors as the best student in pre-law, and that this award was announced at her graduation ceremony. Be careful, however, not to mention awards that are completely irrelevant or outdated. Employers seeking a retail manager, for example, will probably not be interested in a beauty pageant a job seeker won six years ago.

Special Projects

For some fields, such as engineering, aviation, and building construction management, it is essential to include in your cover letter information about special projects you've completed. Your potential employer will want to know exactly what you're capable of doing, and in what capacities you've worked. Remember, however, that the projects you include should be relevant to the position you seek. If you are still a student, feel free to include information about projects you've completed for your courses. The experience many students gain in the classroom is as valid as on-the-job experience, and most employers know this.

To illustrate how to include information about special projects, let's take a student applying for a position as a web consultant. This student has classroom experience working as a web consultant for a local business in her college town. It is useful to feature knowledge of a company, as it will show you've done your research and you feel you're a good match for the corporation. For example, "Indiana Midwestern Insurance values a commitment to customer satisfaction. My experience shows I can work with people from different backgrounds and cultures, which demonstrates that I know how to put customer satisfaction first."

However, we advise you not to let knowledge of a company overwhelm your cover letter. You have very little space to show why you are the best person for the job, and it is best to use this space to focus on transferable skills, accomplishments, awards, and special projects.

Closing

Your closing reveals what you plan to do after your readers have received your resume and cover letter. We recommend you do the following in your closing:

— Inform your readers when you will contact them.

— Include your phone number and e-mail address.

— Thank your readers for their consideration.

A sample closing follows.

> I will contact you before June 5th to discuss my application. I look forward to speaking with you at that time. If you wish to contact me, I may be reached at 765-555-6473, or by e-mail at Thank you for your time and consideration.

This approach may seem bold at first; you may be wondering why you should contact potential employers rather than wait for them to call you. We recommend this approach because potential employers will read your employment materials with more interest if they know you will be calling. Another reason is that many employment professionals prefer candidates who take the initiative to call.

Most importantly, we endorse this approach because it is imperative to follow up on every company that receives your employment materials. Otherwise, your resume and cover letter may end up filed away by the department of human resources. By following up, you can inform prospective employers you're still interested in the position and discover where you are in the hiring process.

When you tell readers you will contact them, be sure to do so. It will not reflect well on you if you forget to call a potential employer when you said you would. It's best to demonstrate your punctuality and interest in the company by calling when you say you will.

Checking

Always proofread your cover letter carefully. After you've finished it, put it aside for a couple of days, and then reread it. You'll be sure to discover sentences that could be improved, or grammatical errors that could otherwise prove to be uncharacteristic of your writing abilities.

Sample Cover Letters

Letter of Inquiry

IM A. SAMPLE
1234 North 55 Street
Believe, Nebraska 68005
402) 292-2345

(Current Date)

Mary Peterson, Manager
Accounting Department
XYZ Company
10 Dear Park Drive
Omaha, Nebraska 68102

Dear Ms. Peterson:

I am writing to introduce myself to you at the suggestion of Professor Johne's of Bellevue University. He has indicated to me that you are very interested in talking to senior Accounting students regarding possible career opportunities.

As you can see in the enclosed resume, I have a very strong academic background in Accounting combined with over five years work experience in accounting and bookkeeping. My recent internship at Mutual of Omaha allowed me to further develop and strengthen my technical and analytical/problem solving skills through the successful completion of a major project involving the conversion of a manual to a computerised accounting system. As Professor Johne's indicated that this type of conversion is a major concern for your organisation over the next year, I believe that I could make a significant and valuable contribution on that project, as well as other challenges that I'm sure you are facing.

I would appreciate the opportunity to discuss how my education and experience are consistent with your needs and will be contacting you within the next few days to talk about the possibility of arranging an interview. Thank you for your time and consideration.

Sincerely,

Jim A. Sam
Enclosure

Letter of Application

4321 South 55 Street
Bellevue, Nebraska 68005
(402) 291-5432

(Current Date)

Mr. John Smith, Director
Marketing and Public Relations
National Non-profit Association
1234 Farnam Street
Omaha, Nebraska 68112

Dear Mr. Smith:

I am applying for the Marketing/Public Relations Intern position advertised through Career Services at Bellevue University. As shown in the enclosed resume, I have a strong academic background in Business Administration and expect to graduate in May, 19xx.

My current work as Advertising Coordinator for our monthly student newspaper has given me first-hand experience in the challenges associated with the development and implementation of a successful marketing/advertising campaign. In addition, I have excellent creative writing and communication skills, as demonstrated by my successful experience in the publication of a weekly in-house newsletter while at Guarantee Mutual.

This background, combined with over five years of general business experience, has given me a unique perspective that would be particularly valuable in meeting the responsibilities of this position, as described in your advertisement. I would welcome the opportunity to meet with you to discuss this position and my qualifications in more detail and look forward to hearing from you soon.

Thank you for your time and consideration.

Sincerely,

Jim A. Sam
Enclosure

Response to Advertisement

IM A. SAMPLE III
3456 Westview Road
Bellevue, Nebraska 68005
Home: (402) 291-5678
Work: (402) 345-1234

(Current Date)

Manager, Human Resources
Tele-marketing Corporation
12123 West Centre Road
Omaha, Nebraska 68134

Dear Human Resources Manager:

I am applying for the position of Customer Service Manager, as advertised in the April 28 issue of the *Omaha World Herald.* With over five years experience in customer service and a strong educational background in human resources management, I believe I could make a significant contribution in helping Tele-marketing Corporation achieve its customer service goals and objectives.

As an example of my most recent accomplishments, I designed and implemented an incentive program that significantly increased productivity among customer service employees which, in turn, significantly raised the level of customer satisfaction with the service provided. Because employee productivity and customer satisfaction are key components of a successful customer service operation, I believe that my expertise in these areas would be of particular value in meeting the challenges of this position.

The enclosed resume summarises the full range of my skills and qualifications. I would appreciate the opportunity for a personal interview to discuss this position and my qualifications in more detail and look forward to hearing from you at your earliest convenience.

Thank you for your consideration.

Sincerely,

Jim A. Sam
Enclosure

Response to Online Advertisement

Peggy S. Smith

762 Ridge Road

Lafayette, IN 47905

peggysmith843@e-mail-link.com

765-555-8493

June 21, 2001

Nancy Thompson, Human Resources Manager

Galavant Group

374 Tomsdale Ave.

Chicago, IL 60614

Dear Ms. Thompson:

As an experienced professional in the building service contracting industry, I am applying for the position of Customer Service Manager, advertised on your website A successful background in the areas of customer service and operations would make me a valuable asset to your company. Providing quality customer service is a major focus of my present position with MKC Associates.

Galavant Group is known as a topnotch company in many areas, especially customer service. I would like to put my customer service experience to work for you. As we both know, it is a competitive market today, and superior customer service is what makes the difference. Managing a customer base of 75 facilities throughout Indiana for the past seven years has sharpened my customer service skills tremendously.

In the last seven years, our employee turnover rate has gone from 150% to 55%. Part of that can be attributed to the development and recognition programs I have instituted, including Christmas parties and summer picnics. Employees need to feel they are part of a "team," and at Galavant Group, that would be one of my goals. Six years ago, I set a personal goal to continue my education at Pursue University.

In December of this year, that goal will be achieved, and I will receive a Bachelor of Science in Organisational Leadership and Supervision. I am proud of this accomplishment, as I have worked full-time while attending Pursue part-time; my GPA is 3.6/4.0. My skills with Galavant Group would be a great opportunity for me to take on a new challenge while fulfilling my commitment to customer service.

I am anxious to talk with you and discuss my potential to contribute to your organisation. I will contact you in three days to discuss my application. You can reach me at 765-555-8493, or by mail at peggysmith843@e-mail-link.com. Thank you for your time and consideration.

Sincerely,

Peggy S. Smith

Address

Enclosure

WRITING RESUMES

The resume is a selling tool that outlines your skills and experiences so an employer can see, at a glance, how you can contribute to the employer's workplace. Your resume has to sell you in short order. While you may have all the requirements for a particular position, your resume is a failure if the employer does not instantly come to the conclusion that you "have what it takes." The first hurdle your resume has to pass—whether it ends up in the "consider file" or the "reject file"—may take less than thirty seconds. The most effective resumes are clearly focused on a specific job title and address the employer's stated requirements for the position. The more you know about the duties and skills required for the job—and organise your resume around these points—the more effective the resume.

Parts of a Resume

Resumes can be divided into three sections: the heading, the body, and the conclusion. Each of these sections has fairly common contents.

Heading

The top third of the resume is the heading. It contains your name, phone numbers, address, and other details such as your occupation, titles, and so on. Some resume writers include the name of their profession, occupation, or field. In some examples, you'll see writers putting things like "CERTIFIED PHYSICAL THERAPIST" very prominently in the heading. Headings can also contain a goals and objectives subsection and a highlights subsection. These two special subsections are described later in "Special Sections in Resumes."

Body

In a one-page resume, the body is the middle portion, taking up a half or more of the total space of the resume. In this section, you present the details of your work, education, and military experience. This information is arranged in reverse chronological order. In the body section, you also include your accomplishments, for example, publications, certifications, equipment you are familiar with, and so on. There are many ways to present this information:

— You can divide it functionally—into separate sections for work experience and education.

— You can divide it thematically—into separate sections for the different areas of your experience and education.

Conclusion

In the final third or quarter of the resume, you can present other related information on your background. For example, you can list activities, professional associations, memberships, hobbies, and interests. At the bottom of the resume, people often put “REFERENCES AVAILABLE ON REQUEST” and the date of preparation of the resume.

At first, you might think that listing non-work and personal information would be totally irrelevant and inappropriate. Actually, it can come in handy—it personalises you to potential employers and gives you something to chat while you’re waiting for the coffee machine or the elevator. For example, if you mention in your resume that you raise goats, that gives the interviewer something to chat with you about during those moments of otherwise uncomfortable silence.

Types of Resumes

Putting together a resume is very serious business. Often it is the first impression you will make on a prospective employer. After looking over your resume, the employer will grant you the opportunity to make a second impression. When putting together your resume, evaluate the needs of the employer and then determine how you can fill those needs. If you have access to a computer and a quality printer, you can design a targeted resume for every job for which you apply. If you have to mass produce your resume, you will have to do a little guesswork to come up with one that will impress everyone. There are three basic types: chronological, functional, and a combination of the two.

Chronological Resume

The chronological resume is probably the one with which most people are familiar. On it, work experience is listed in reverse chronological order (most recent job first). The period of time during which you were employed is listed first, followed by the name of the employer and then the employer’s location. A description for each job is also included. Following work history is a section on education. If you are trying to show career growth, a chronological resume may be the way to go. If your most recent job is store manager, while the one before that is department manager, and the one before that is sales clerk, you can show a history of promotion. However, if your work history has been spotty or if it has been stagnant you shouldn’t use a chronological resume. If you are changing careers, a chronological resume is not for you either.

Outline

What follows is an outline of a typical chronological resume—best suited for entry-level job-seekers or those who have stayed in the same field. Career changers and those job-seekers with varied work experiences and accomplishments may want to utilise a functional resume style. Here are the key components of a standard chronological resume:

— *Identification.* It is essential that a potential employer can reach you.

  This section should include your name, address, phone number(s), and e-mail address. If a college student, this section might also include a school address and a permanent home address.

— *Job Objective.* A job objective is optional and should only be included for new college grade and those changing careers. Otherwise, use your cover letter to show your career interests and job objective.

  If you do use an objective, make sure your objective explains the kind of work you want to do, and keep it between two to four typed lines.

— *Key Accomplishments.* Some resume experts are suggesting adding a section that highlights your key accomplishments and achievements. Think of this section as an executive summary of your resume; identify key accomplishments that will grab the attention of an employer.

— *Education.* For new college grade, this entry should be your next. For others with full-time work experience, this section should follow your experience section.

  This section should include school(s) attended (including years of attendance), majors/minors, degrees, and honours and awards received.

  For new grade only: There appears to be a growing trend of employers wanting your GPA in this section. If you decide to do so, make sure to use the GPA that puts you in the best light—either overall GPA, school or college GPA, or major GPA.

— *Professional Experience*. This section can also be labelled "Experience, "Work History," or "Employment." We like using experience—especially for new college grade, because experience is broader than work history, allowing you to include major school projects that showcase your skills and abilities.

This section should include company name, your job title, dates of employment, and major accomplishments. List experiences in reverse chronological order, starting with your most current experience.

List your accomplishments in bullet format (rather than paragraph format). Avoid discussing job duties or responsibilities.

If you don't have a lot of career-related job experience, consider using transferable skills to better highlight your work experience.

Finally, make sure to make use of action verbs when describing your accomplishments.

— *Affiliations/Interests*. This section is optional; include only if you have room on your resume for it. Items from this section are often used as an icebreaker by interviewers looking to start an interview on an informal basis.

This section should only include professional memberships and noncontroversial activities/interests.

— *References*. Many experts say this section is passe, but if you have room, include it. If nothing else, this section signals the end of your resume.

This section should only include a statement saying references are available upon request.

Do not include the names of your references on your resume.

Functional Resume

A functional resume categorises skills by function, emphasising your abilities. This is useful if you are changing careers and want to show how you can transfer your skills. As stated previously, it is important to show prospective employers what you can offer them. A functional resume does just that. A functional job objective is given first, followed by several paragraphs, each discussing a different job function.

Examples of functions are: Supervision and Management, Accounting, and Writing and Editing. Begin with the one you want to emphasise most. If you are customising your resume for different employers, you can change your functional job objective as well as the order in which you list the functions. However, if you don't list your previous jobs, the person reviewing your resume may be suspicious.

Among job seekers who should consider a functional format:

— Those with very diverse experiences that don't add up to a clear-cut career path.

— College students with minimal experience and/or experience unrelated to their chosen career field.

— Career-changers who wish to enter a field very different from what all their previous experience points to.

— Those with gaps in their work history, such as homemakers who took time to raise and family and now wish to return to the workplace. For them, a chronological format can draw undue attention to those gaps, while a functional resume enables them to portray transferable skills attained through such activities as domestic management and volunteer work.

— Military transitioners entering a different field from the work they did in the military.

— Job-seekers whose predominate or most relevant experience has been unpaid, such as volunteer work or college activities (course work, class projects, extracurricular organisations, and sports).

— Those who performed very similar activities throughout their past jobs who want to avoid repeating those activities in a chronological job listing.

— Job-seekers looking for a position for which a chronological listing would make them look "over qualified."

— Older workers seeking to de-emphasise a lengthy job history.

If you can look at a chronological resume without a stated career objective and know exactly what field the job seeker is headed toward and would be good at, then the chronological format probably is working just fine. But if you can't guess what the job seeker wants to do and would be good at by looking at the chronology of past jobs, a functional format may be indicated.

The functional format also can work well for college students because it allows skills attained from experiences other than paid employment to be listed within the skills clusters.

Functional formats have been the subject of some employer backlash is recent years. Some employers are unaccustomed to the functional format, and they may become confused or even irritated by functional resumes. Recruiters/headhunters particularly disdain functional formats, so this approach should never be used if you are primarily targeting recruiters with your job search. Employers in conservative fields, such as banking, finance, and law are not big fans of functional formats, nor are international employers.

Functional formats also are not acceptable on many online job boards. Some employers like to know what you did in each job. One solution is to structure your resume in a mostly functional format but include a bare-bones work history in reverse chronological order, creating what is variously known as a chorion-functional, hybrid, or combination format. Such a work-history section need include only job title, name and location of employer, and dates of employment.

To make your functional resume as reader-friendly as possible for employers, include as much context as you can within each functional description. That way, the employer has a better idea of which skill aligns with which job. In the above leadership-skills example, for instance, the student tells where she demonstrated each skill, thus making helping the employer connect her skills with the experience that produced those skills.

Sample of a Functional Resume

MARY A. HOMEMAKER
5555 East Main Circle Elmira,
NY 55555 (555) 111-0000

OBJECTIVE

Clerical/Bookkeeping/Office Support position

SUMMARY OF QUALIFICATIONS

— Outstanding math skills; enjoy working with figures.

— Knowledge of clerical details, record and file maintenance.

— Strong background in all aspects of customer service and support.

— Excellent organisational, planning, interpersonal and communications skills.

SKILLS AND ABILITIES

Bookkeeping:

— Responsible for all accounts receivable and payable functions as auditor for hotel operation.

— Prepared daily, monthly, and yearly balance sheets for auditing purposes.

— Oversaw daily cash control, prepared bank and credit card deposits.

— Collected payments for customer billing and posted to general ledger.

Clerical:

— Posted all room, tax, vale, long-distance and restaurant charges to house guests' individual accounts.

— Prepared comprehensive housekeeping report for Head Housekeeper.

— Utilised computer to schedule reservations around the work for guests.

Customer Service:

— Handled customer inquiries and complaints in a professional manner.

— Adept at handling confrontational situations, resolving them appropriately.

— Communicated with guests and customers via switchboard operation.

Management:

— Scheduled, trained and supervised staff arriving for daily shift.

— Supervised and oversaw security of building, including physical plant.

— Oversaw all hotel operations and guest relations as management staff.

EXPERIENCE

Clerk/ Bookkeeper	Elmira Conference Centre	Elmira, New York
Desk Clerk	Happy Town Hotel	Elmira, New York

Secretary/ Production Clerk	Elmira Manufacturing Company	Elmira, New York
Job Cost Clerk	Binghamton Mailing (Mail Order Dept.)	Binghamton, New York

EDUCATION/TRAINING

— Business Administration Program - Pursue University Extension, Pursue, New York

— Associate's Degree, Secretarial Science - Elmira Technical College, Elmira, New York

— Graduate - Anywhere High School, Anywhere, New York

ACTIVITIES/INTERESTS

— Volunteer: Travel & Tourism (Information Centre), Anywhere County Chamber of Commerce;

— Anywhere Soup Kitchen, Anywhere, New York

— Past Instructor of Quilting Program, James Human Resource Centre, James, New York

— Past Girl Scout Leader

REFERENCES

Available upon request

Combination Resume

A combination resume is exactly what it sounds like—it combines a functional resume with a chronological one. An objective is listed at the top, after your name and address, of course. Following that are paragraphs describing job functions. A section titled "Employment Experience" comes next. That is where the chronological part of the resume comes in. List employers and dates in this section. Do not offer further descriptions here as you have already described your abilities in the functional part of this resume. This is a useful format if you are changing careers but have a solid employment history. If you spent a long time at one job but moved up through the company, you might want to use a combination resume. Combination resume will be of best to use when:

— Jobs and activity titles are not directly related to the career goals
— Applying for different positions requiring the same skill
— Your titles are impressive, but may be unrelated

Sample of Combination Resume

NAME
1021 Main Street
Green Bay, WI 54301
920-462-7689

OBJECTIVE:

An entry-level position leading to a career in investment or financial analysis using analytical, organisational, and communication skills.

EDUCATION:

University of Wisconsin- Green Bay, Green Bay, Wisconsin, BA in Psychology, May 1999, GPA 3.4/4.0

ANALYTICAL SKILLS:

Reporter, Fourth Estate, University of Wisconsin-Green Bay

Developed strategies for interviewing and article-writing. Planned best approach to take in presentation of issue. 9/98-6/99

Student Manager, Chartwells, University Wisconsin-Green Bay

Managed banquet and catering services. Assessed and solved operational problems. Introduced more efficient methods of operation. Recruited and trained new workers. 1/98-present

ORGANISATIONAL SKILLS:

Hostess, Country Inn and Suites, Green Bay, Wisconsin

Coordinated waitresses and scheduled break times. Handled cash and credit payments. Planned customer-seating patterns. Winter break 1997

Organiser and Creator, House cleaning Service, Green Bay, Wisconsin

Instituted a local house cleaning service. Devised advertising scheme. Developed efficient cleaning routine. 6/97-8/97

COMMUNICATION SKILLS:

Public Relations Office Assistant, Alumni Affairs, University of Wisconsin - Green Bay

Acquired public relations abilities through alumni communications. Designed reunion weekend signs and posters. 3/98-6/98

Telephone Solicitor, ITI Marketing, Green Bay, Wisconsin

Developed sales ability and good telephone personality. Achieved award-winning sales. Acquired efficient sales approach and voice. Winter break 1997

REFERENCES:

Available upon request

Bibliography

Alison Baverstock, *Publicity, Newsletters, and Press Releases*, Oxford: Oxford University Press, 2002.

Bryan A. Garner. 1991. *The Elements of Legal Style.* Oxford University Press,

Carey C.V., *Mind the Stop: A brief guide to punctuation and a note on proof-correction*, first published Cambridge University Press, 1939.

Charles T. Brusaw et al, *Handbook of Technical Writing*, Fifth Edition, New York: St. Martin's Press, 1997.

Christian W. Dawson, *The Essence of Computing Projects - A Student's Guide*, London: Prentice Hall, 2000.

Christopher Callahan, *A Journalist's Guide to the Internet: the net as a reporting tool*, Boston: Allyn and Bacon, 1999.

Claire Kehrwald Cook, *Line by Line: How to improve your own writing*, Houghton Mifflin, 1986.

Daniel Anderson, Bret Benjamin, Bill Paredes-Holt, *Connections: a guide to on-line writing*, Boston: Allyn and Bacon, 1998.

Daniel Anderson, Bret Benjamin, Bill Paredes-Holt, *Connections: a guide to on-line writing*, Boston: Allyn and Bacon, 1998.

David Mellinkoff, 1982. *Legal Writing: Sense & Nonsense.* West Publishing Company.

Edward R. Tufte, 1983. *The Visual Display of Quantitative Information* Graphics Press.

Fayol, M., Largy, P., & Lemaire, P. (1994). When cognitive overload enhances subject-verb agreement errors. *Quarterly Journal of Experimental Psychology, 47A*, 437-464.

Feldman, D. H. 1986. *Nature's gambit: Child prodigies and the development of human potential*. New York: Basic Books.

Fowler, H. W.; Burchfield, R. W. *The New Fowler's Modern English Usage* (Third, revised ed.). Oxford: Oxford University Press. p. 162. 2000.

Galbraith, D. 1999. Writing as a knowledge-constituting process. In M. Torrance, & D. Galbraith (Eds.), *Studies in writing: Vol. 4. Knowing what to write: Conceptual processes in text production* (pp. 139-160). Amsterdam: Amsterdam University Press.

Gerald J. Alred et al, *The Professional Writer*, New York: St Martin's Press, 1992.

Gibaldi, Joseph. *MLA Handbook for Writers of Research Papers*. New York: Modern Language Association, 2003.

Gowers, Ernest. *Plain Words: a guide to the use of English*. London: Her Majesty's Stationery Office. 1948.

Hayes, J. R. 2004. What triggers revision? In L. Allal, L. Chanquoy, & P. Largy (Eds.), *Revision of written language: Cognitive and instructional processes* (pp. 9-20). Boston/Dordrecht, Netherlands/New York: Kluwer.

Henry, J. 2000. *Writing workplace cultures: An archeology of professional writing*. Carbondale, IL: Southen Illinois University Press.

Howard S. Becker, *Tricks of the Trade: how to think about our research while you're doing it*, University of Chicago Press, 1998.

Hy Bender, *Essential Software for Writers: a complete guide for everyone who writes with a PC*, Cincinnati, OH: Writer's Digest Books, 1993.

Ives, George B. *Text, Type and Style: A Compendium of Atlantic Usage*. Boston: Atlantic Monthly Press. 1921.

Jarvie, Gordon. *Chambers Punctuation Guide*. Edinburgh: Chambers. 1992.

Jo Billingham, *Editing and Revising Text*, Oxford: Oxford University Press, 2002.

John Clancy and Brigid Ballard, *How to Write Essays: A practical guide for students*, Longman Cheshire, 1983.

Johnstone, K. M., Ashbaugh, H., & Warfield, T. D. (2002). Effects of repeated practice and contextual-writing experiences on college students' writing skills. *Journal of Educational Psychology, 94*, 305-315.

Jonathan Anderson and Millicent Poole, *Thesis and Assignment Writing*, London: John Wiley, 1994.

Jonathan Anderson and Millicent Poole, *Thesis and Assignment Writing*, London: John Wiley, 1994.

Judd, Karen. *Copyediting: A Practical Guide*. Menlo Park, Calif: Crisp Publications. 2001.

Judith Bell, *Doing Your Research Project: A Guide for First-Time Researchers in Education and Social Science*, Buckingham: Open University Press (2nd edn) 1993.

Karen Elizabeth Gordon, 1984. *The Transitive Vampire: A Handbook* of Grammar for the Innocent, the Eager, and the Doomed . Times Books.

Loberger, Gordon; Kate Shoup Welsh. *Webster's new world English grammar handbook.* New York: Hungry Minds. 2001.

Lorraine Blaxter et al, *How to Research*, Buckingham: Open University Press, (second edition) 2001.

Lorraine Blaxter et al, *How to Research*, Buckingham: Open University Press, (second edition) 2001.

Lynne Truss, *Eats, Shoots and Leaves*, Gotham Books. 2004.

Martin Cutts, *Oxford Guide to Plain English*, Oxford: Oxford University Press, 2004.

Naomi S. Baron, *Alphabet to Email: How Written English* Evolved and Where It's Heading, London/New York: Routledge, 2000.

Parkes, Malcolm Beckwith. *Pause and Effect: An Introduction to the History of Punctuation in the West*. University of California Press. 1993.

Phyllis Creme and Mary R.Lea, *Writing* at *University: a guide for students*, Buckingham: Open University Press, 1997.

Ralph Berry, *The Research Project: how to write it*, Routledge, third edition, 1994.

Richard C. Wydick, 1985. *Plain English for Lawyers.* Carolina Academic Press.

Rita S. Brause, *Writing* your Doctoral Dissertation: Invisible Rules for Success, London and New York: Falmer Press, 2000.

Ritter, R.M. The Oxford Guide to Style. Oxford University Press. p. 140. 2002.

Robert Barrass, *Students Must Write: A Guide to Better Writing in Coursework and Examinations,* London: Routledge, second edition 1995.

Robin Williams, 1990. *The Mac Is Not a Typewriter.* Peachpit Press.

Tom Goldstein and Jethro K. Lieberman, 1989. *The LawyerÕs Guide* to Writing Well. University of California Press.

Truss, Lynne. *Eats, Shoots & Leaves: The Zero Tolerance Approach to Punctuation*, 2003. Gotham Books, Toronto.

Wells, J. C. *Accents of English*, 3 vols. Cambridge: Cambridge University Press. 1982.

William Condon and Wayne Butler, *Writing the Information SuperHighway,* Boston: Allyn and Bacon, 1997.